MW01630456

STRUCTURE + Design

Morgante Wilson Architects, page 203

signature work by leading architects and interior designers

Panache Partners, LLC
PO Box 797126
Dallas, TX 75379
469.246.6060
www.panache.com

Publishers: Brian G. Carabet and John A. Shand
Regional Publisher: Marc Zurba
Managing Editor: Rosalie Wilson
Editor: Megan Winkler
Editor: Lori Tate
Editor: Rachel Watkins
Art Director: Brian Carabet
Administrative Coordinator: Susan Minner

Printed in Malaysia

Distributed by Independent Publishers Group
800.888.4741

PUBLISHER'S DATA

Structure + Design

Library of Congress Control Number: 2016912485

ISBN 13: 978-0-9969653-5-4

First Printing 2016

10 9 8 7 6 5 4 3 2 1

STRUCTURE + Design

signature work by leading architects and interior designers

Dean Larkin Design, page 235

Neal Prince Studio, page 83

INTRODUCTION

Balance, movement, proportion, rhythm: Design is artistry built for people's lives. The undeniably human element of architecture and design is a two-way street and only the best-of-the-best master the balance of communication, collaboration, and creativity. To extract the essence of a homeowner's personality, how he or she lives their everyday lives, architects and designers must embark on a journey of discovery and partnership with the owner. The process requires knowledge of multiple disciplines, enthusiasm to persevere overtime, the keen ability to innovate with new technology and methods, and communicate with myriad personalities.

At times arduous, and others surprising, each project demands that the architect, designer, builder, and the rest of the carefully curated team pour their energy into transforming imagination into reality. Ensuring that each space has its own flavor and personality, that it flows into adjacent rooms, and that it fits the needs of the people who will call those rooms home, these experts create private sanctuaries and entertaining spaces that delight.

Structure + Design features the impressive work of professionals from diverse backgrounds, who effortlessly meet all the challenges of architecture and design to express a sense of style that's as unique as the people who call on them to build their homes. This book lays the foundation for inspiration through stunning images that present an insider's look into unparalleled homes, and gives you the inside story on exactly what goes into building a timeless residence.

JLF Design Build, page 281

CONTENTS

SOUTHEAST

NORTHEAST

MIDWEST

WEST

"All fine architectural values are human values, else not valuable."

—Frank Lloyd Wright

Pepe Calderin Design, page 87

CHAPTER ONE

Monogram Builders, page 75

Camens Architectural Group, page 19

Southeast

BENTLEY THE BOOK

AKSEIZER DESIGN GROUP

ALEXANDRIA, VA

If every space tells a story, it is the interior designer's responsibility to create a compelling narrative. That's exactly what Jeff Akseizer, principal of Akseizer Design Group, does each time he embarks on a new project. He considers the interior views, the progression of light, the flow of space, as well as the client's stylistic sensibilities. Each design unfolds through a curated collection of innovative materials and sumptuous textures, delicately balanced and impeccably executed down to the most finely stitched detail. During the creation of each exquisite environment, ADG's diverse team of interior design, architecture, and branding professionals are deeply engaged in every facet of the project, whether commercial or residential. As lifestyle tastemakers, Jeff and his team collaborate closely with their clients to envision signature spaces that are as vibrant as they are versatile, often yielding results that far exceed expectations.

Established in 2006, ADG has extensive experience and a dynamic portfolio of multi-family, hospitality, commercial, and luxury residential properties within the greater Washington, DC and New York regions, and throughout North America. ADG also owns and operates an elite millwork factory in Boswell, Pennsylvania, which offers in-house production for many of the beautiful custom case goods that adorn their projects.

"All the elements of a room must weave together to tell a story; following the flow of life, there is a beginning, a middle, and an end."

—Jeff Akseizer

ABOVE: At Silo Point, an innovative adaptive reuse design transformed a historic industrial grain elevator into luxury condominium residences that boast stunning 360-degree views of Baltimore Harbor. Designers Jeff Akseizer and Jamie Brown kept the penthouse light and open to capitalize on the unparalleled outlook through the soaring curtain window walls. The glass and steel staircase continues the open concept and allows for seamless movement between floors without obstructing the remarkable view.
Photograph by Virtuance

FACING PAGE: The dining area is beautifully dressed and inviting. A dynamic chandelier hovers above the sculptural glass and acrylic table, while a subtly textured wallcovering grounds the space in warmth and comfort.
Photograph by April Greer

PREVIOUS PAGES: The incomparable penthouse at Silo Point emerged as a jewel box in the sky, with scenic harbor views framing the voluminous great room. Generous coffee tables and spacious seating allows guests to gather flexibly throughout the space, accented by a striking geometric rug and plush velvet pillows. Custom lighting and bespoke draperies soften the structural columns and echo the room's impressive scale.
Photograph by Virtuance

"Design should be fun for the homeowner. As a designer, it's our job to discover what 'fun' means to each client."

—Jeff Akseizer

ABOVE: A seductive wine lounge replete with polished natural elements evokes the outdoors. Behind the bar, an illuminated onyx slab brings a warm glow to this generous alcove. Tailored seating atop a herringbone floor invites residents to unwind and entertain. Impeccable environments of this caliber evolve through extensive collaboration within ADG's design team, which includes Lindsay Pavliga, Lina Aldana, Katy Fries, Ginger Teapole, Crystal Smittkamp, Marie Jilson, Sonya Lim, and architecture principal Gozde Tanyeri.
Photograph courtesy of ADG/Akseizer Design Group

FACING PAGE: The Lauren Residences boasts 29 exclusive estates in the heart of downtown Bethesda, Maryland. The formal living room features custom bookshelves and a layered tonal palette that breathes fresh elegance into the transitional design. Supple window treatments welcome ample light into the serene space and create an environment of modern comfort.
Photographs courtesy of April Greer

"Luxury design is a reflection of one's personal lifestyle, every element should be well-made and well-deserved."

—Jeff Akseizer

ABOVE LEFT: A contemporary acrylic box contains a classical bust, unpredictably situated atop a modern fashion volume. The artful arrangement of this striking composition elicits playful visual tension, frequently sparking conversation on artifacts old and new.
Photograph by Angie Seckinger

ABOVE MIDDLE: Natural elements abound in this soothing space that invites guests to linger. Collectibles from all eras nest side by side, and comfort reigns supreme on a custom-made sectional, bedecked with plush pillows.
Photograph by Angie Seckinger

ABOVE RIGHT: A stylish acrylic table and a vintage Dutch chair enhance a quiet nook under the eave. The alcove comes to life with an original artwork by a local children's hospital patient. The balance of fine furnishings and whimsical decor begets an approachable yet stylish appeal.
Photograph by Angie Seckinger

FACING PAGE: Akseizer and Brown infused natural textures throughout a traditional dining space, creating a seamless canopy of birch branches within a coffered ceiling. Imperfection is perfection for this collection of luxe organic elements and rich textures that offers a feast for the eyes. Ethically-sourced cowhides adorn the chairs surrounding an elegant dining table, dressed in Anna Weatherley fine china. A sculptural light fixture and custom cabinetry by ADG millwork add sophisticated flair to this intimate gathering space.
Photograph by April Greer

CAMENS ARCHITECTURAL GROUP

CHARLESTON, SC

When building homes in a beautiful setting, homeowners and many architects focus on the outdoors and bringing them in. Marc Camens, principal and founder of Camens Architectural Group, chooses to build homes in the opposite way, and the results are absolutely spectacular. Marc builds homes from the inside out by first learning about how his clients live, rather than developing a laundry list of rooms and features. He learns how they eat, entertain, cook, relax, and work at home. Then he considers the site and adapts the floorplan—based on the owners' lifestyles—to the site to integrate the two. Finally, he builds the exterior around the plan to envelop it. According to Marc, when an architect builds in the opposite way—taking the exterior into consideration first—they risk stuffing the interiors with rooms that the owners do not need.

It is with this approach in mind that Marc leads his team of architects to build distinctive residences that are classically Southern and immediately feel like home. Homeowners are guided through every step of the design and building process, and love watching their visions come to life. Fine details, from intricate millwork and decorative columns that transition one between spaces, to leaded glass accents and even accent lighting in kitchen cabinetry, are taken into account by the architects of Camens Architectural Group. The homes that result are breathtaking, well-built, and memorable, holding true to the firm's unofficial slogan: listen to your dreams and we'll listen to you.

"It's vitally important for the energy and light to continue to flow throughout each space."

—Marc Camens

ABOVE: A stunning array of windows make the back of the home an incredible sight after the sun goes down. Multiple vantage points throughout the floorplan offer ample ways to view the island. Out back, the patio steps down to the keyhole-shaped pool nestled near the home. Working in conjunction with a landscape architect, the team designed and built a beautiful backyard retreat for the owners and guests.
Photograph by Holger Obenaus

FACING PAGE: The tall ceiling of the living room allows for light to flow freely through the transom windows. Passages to the dining area and bar, the kitchen, and the entryway are grand and define the transition without blocking the flow of energy. Each detail was carefully considered, down to the placement of the window over the kitchen sink to perfectly align with the entry to the living room, and the room itself. The high window above helps to reinforce the symmetry, while lightening the dark ceiling.
Photograph by Holger Obenaus

PREVIOUS PAGES: The Kiawah Island home opens to the beautiful landscape through the use of transom and larger windows throughout. A signature Camens chimney cap adorns the chimney, while the copper roof will age beautifully over time. Although it was intended to be their second home, the owners loved it so much that they made it their primary residence.
Photograph by Rick Smoak

ABOVE: Details make a home special. Designed around the way the family wants to live in the house, the living room is light and airy with intricate details overhead. Lofty windows allow light to flood the space with a soft, ethereal feel. Leaded glass and columns frame the transition between the living room and kitchen. Dark cabinets ground the kitchen, while glass-front upper cabinets and a large window keep the energy flowing.
Photograph by Rick Smoak

FACING PAGE TOP: The shingle-style Kiawah Island home boasts a variety of windows to capture the views of nature. A copper roof that weathers well as it ages adds a touch of elegance. A simple but chic staircase carries visitors to the front door, where many stop to take in the views.
Photograph by Holger Obenaus

FACING PAGE BOTTOM LEFT & BOTTOM RIGHT: Once inside the home, another elegant staircase allows for the free movement of energy and light as one travels between floors. Intricate white-on-white millwork throughout the home elevates each room, giving it a classic look while keeping everything crisp and clean.
Photographs by Holger Obenaus

"Learning about how owners really live gives you the best picture of what their home should be."

—Marc Camens

TOP LEFT: The three-story home is another that was intended to be the owners' secondary home, but when they moved in, they loved it so much that they made it their first residence. Nature and architecture blend beautifully with the towering home, and there isn't a bad view to be had when inside.

MIDDLE LEFT & BOTTOM LEFT: Custom woodwork plays a central role as another way to merge the indoors with the outdoors. While full walls of windows are spread throughout the home, others pop up in unexpected places, such as the diamond-shaped window in the stairway. The home is dynamic and subtly playful.

FACING PAGE TOP: Sweeping rooflines add a flowing gracefulness to the shingle-style home on Kiawah Island. Rows of windows and details like the Camens bracket—a signature element—under the eaves make this home something special.

FACING PAGE BOTTOM: An infinity edge pool is nestled against the back of the home, where the Camens brackets are prominently seen under the eaves. A multitude of windows open the house up to the outdoors and the incredible views. Small details, like the window panes at the top of each large picture window, add interest. Their intentional placement adds a decorative element to each window without interrupting the view.

Photographs by Rick Smoak

CARSON GUEST INTERIOR DESIGN

ATLANTA, GA

Rita Carson Guest, FASID, and John F. Guest, Allied Member ASID, launched their design business in 1984, specializing in law offices. Little did they know that such corporate endeavors would quickly translate to the residential side, as well. Their work made such an impact that many of the law partners and executives were soon asking them to design their own high-rise condominiums and homes. Now, Carson Guest effortlessly balances corporate, institutional, retail, and residential projects while moving between traditional, contemporary, and transitional styles. The award-winning, full-service firm creates value by designing beautiful and functional spaces that help their clients promote their unique brands or personalities while solving challenges along the way.

Whether Carson Guest is planning a work environment to be more comfortable, productive, and aesthetically pleasing, or making a home more dynamic, efficient and inviting, a sense of quality, personalization and integrity is at the backbone of each of the firm's projects. After all, client satisfaction is viewed as the most important product of their work—and creative, detail-oriented ability, and professional service are the tools by which they achieve it.

LEFT: What once was a very traditional home in the John's Creek gated community suburb, north of Atlanta, received a sleek, contemporary update at the hands of Carson Guest. The homeowners commissioned the firm for the project after receiving a similar design transformation at their corporate offices. Using an entirely integrated approach that went way beyond just furnishings and décor, they reconfigured the floorplan to open up the footprint of the kitchen and breakfast area as well as a new family-friendly den, which was formerly an unused sun room. The new floor-to-ceiling windows in the den not only wash the space in natural light but also frame the beautiful view overlooking the pool in the backyard.
Photograph courtesy of Gabriel Benzur

"It's a matter of contrast—the right mix of textures and materials creates a sense of sleek sophistication while being warm and inviting, too."

—Rita Carson Guest

ABOVE LEFT: Echoing the marble used in the living room, the foyer of the Georgian-style home features the black and white polished stone laid in a statement-making starburst design. Additionally, the staircase was reoriented to a seductive, curved shape complete with custom, handmade wrought iron rails.

ABOVE RIGHT: Shades of gray don't have to be cold, as is perfectly demonstrated in this award-winning master bathroom in the John's Creek home. The beautiful grain of Calcutta Manhattan marble walls and a mosaic tile floor melds with the warm gray of the onyx wall in the shower. LED lighting under the shower shelves lends an ambient glow.

FACING PAGE TOP: The crisp contrast between dark, matte wood floors and white woodwork along with Princess White iridescent quartzite provides a striking yet warm finish in the kitchen. The large central island, flanked by bar stools, encourages an open, communal feel. The round breakfast table is handmade and stained in a gray oak finish to echo the color palette of the space.

FACING PAGE BOTTOM: A separate project in Atlanta, the highly traditional, Georgian-style private estate received a modern edge that still celebrated its elegant heritage. In the living room, the 25-foot ceilings are maximized with tall windows that look out to the pool. Floors that were once heavy and casual with terra cotta tiles were replaced with glossy, black and white marble, laid in a geometric square pattern. A custom handmade floral rug provides a lush, warm finish.

Photographs courtesy of Carson Guest and Gabriel Benzur

"Good design must always have value; it should provide comfort, nurture creativity, and foster physical and emotional wellness."

—Rita Carson Guest

ABOVE: Once a small, dark area with no natural light, this living area in the John's Creek home took on a far more pleasant and functional experience. Glass walls visually connect the space to the kitchen and breakfast area and bring an airy sense of light into the small room. The main focal point of the space, though, is the Calcutta Manhattan marble fireplace, which might as well be a work of art with its expertly aligned grain and striations. It's flanked by white, lacquered cabinets on each side, which are inspired by the high-gloss polish of the stone. Counteracting the linear lines of the fireplace, a round, custom leather ottoman and curved club chairs bring softness back into the space while the handmade rug features a subtle zebra print for a bit of visual stimulation—from the ground up.

FACING PAGE: A hallway bar area paves a path between the formal dining room and the kitchen in the John's Creek property. Architectural millwork and doorway arches were added, framing the view of the farm sink and the windows facing out to the backyard. A concealed pantry on the left of the hallway is disguised with mirrors, which visually expand the space even more and reflect the radiant glow of the custom lighting.

Photographs courtesy of Gabriel Benzur

CHRISTOPHER ROSE ARCHITECTS

JOHNS ISLAND, SC

Refraining from common style, Christopher Rose Architects approaches each project as a unique expression of their clients' personality and way of life. The small, collaborative design firm focuses on the design pillars of detail, clarity, tradition, and innovation as they develop a unique identity for each home. At the core, though, is a design philosophy that's deeply entrenched in South Carolina's rich architectural history and dynamic landscape while integrating ever-evolving technological advances and modern appeal.

Christopher Rose Architects sites each property carefully, taking into account such factors as the sun, breeze, air flow, and surrounding views. Their homes value efficiency, spatial simplicity, and clarity, all of which serve to create a retreat from the hustle and bustle of daily life. Also at the foundation of the firm is a commitment to sustainable design while never compromising the utmost attention to detail.

The award-winning team has worked together for many years, so they not only bring a spirit of close collaboration but also a wide variety of expertise and knowledge to every project. Through a steady dialogue and understanding between client and architect, they customize each and every design plan and create homes that marry the traditions of the past with their signature vision and specificity.

"It is essential to cultivate an awareness of regional traditions coupled with contemporary advances to produce homes with lasting, distinct appeal."

—Christopher Rose

ABOVE LEFT: Located on the northern end of Kiawah Island, the Blue Heron Pond home is a contemporary marvel that enjoys uninterrupted lagoon views and uncompromising privacy. Like a breath of fresh air, the home's open-plan great room blurs the line between interior and exterior with soaring 30-foot glass walls featuring hurricane- and noise-resistant windows, a Douglas fir ceiling, stained bamboo flooring, and a 26-foot North Carolina blue stone fireplace.
Photograph by Rion Rizzo Creative Resources Photography

ABOVE RIGHT: The master suite makes an impact with its soaring walls of glass and a vaulted ceiling that includes a custom-built valance and cove lighting. Automated shades allow for privacy without compromising the clean, crisp aesthetic.
Photograph by Rion Rizzo Creative Resources Photography

FACING PAGE: High-tech meets low-country at the property; it simultaneously stretches the architectural imagination while remaining an easy, livable atmosphere that embraces Kiawah's spectacular natural setting. The back of the residence features vast expanses of glass to maximize the views.
Photograph by Rion Rizzo Creative Resources Photography

PREVIOUS PAGES: Dramatic curb appeal is instantly achieved in this architectural dynamo of a design that brings statement-making grandeur to low-country roots. The indoor-outdoor lifestyle is fully celebrated with ample, elevated deck space and wraparound porches that extend the interior living areas of the property.
Photograph by Holger Openaus Photography

ITALY OF MY DREAMS
SALADINO VILLA

CINDY MEADOR INTERIORS

GULF SHORES, AL

Fashion and interior design share many basic principles, but it all comes down to presentation and creating for people. It makes sense then that Cindy Meador found her way to the interior design world through fashion. Having worked for many years in the wholesale side of brands like Urban Outfitters and Anthropologie, Cindy decided she wanted to do something different with her life. After spending time in Dallas, Los Angeles, and New York, Cindy returned home to Alabama and opened Cindy Meador Interiors in Gulf Shores.

Combining the vintage and the contemporary, Cindy's designs are a harmonious balance between styles that perfectly reflect the lifestyle of homeowners. Every job is different, but there's one thing that's consistent in Cindy's designs: they're fresh, timeless, and subtly elegant. There's always a touch of glam, but the finesse is in the details for Cindy and nothing is ever overt or overdone. Her 3,000-square-foot design studio is always busy with activity as she and her team sift through design books, catalogs, and samples with clients to create the perfect design for their home. On street level, her retail showroom offers an array of art, furnishings, textiles, and accessories, all with classic Southern charm.

ABOVE LEFT: The homeowners are well-traveled and fell in love with Venice, so the designer opted for a Venetian feel for their master bedroom. A mirrored headboard is the crowning jewel of the room that epitomizes Old World luxury. The bedside commode tables were handcrafted and hand-painted specifically for the space and perfectly match the soft color palette of the room. A light blue Venetian chandelier hangs overhead, and the Venetian plaster was hand-plastered by a fifth-generation Italian plaster craftsman from Louisiana.

ABOVE RIGHT: The side entrance of the home features a beautiful staircase. The antique Indian bone-inlay table is flanked by two Empire chairs that can be pulled up to the dining table when more seating is needed. The combination of the Fortuny fabric on the chairs and the Italian intaglios on the wall behind creates a clean but classic look for the lofty entrance.

PREVIOUS PAGES: With such a large space to work with, the designer didn't want the joined living and dining area to feel cold or unwelcoming. When entering the home, the eye is immediately drawn to the arched windows that look out onto the loggia and pool beyond, so it made sense to optimize that view. Combining low-profile pieces like the Italian leather sofa, the French bergére chairs, and low-back Baker chairs ensures that the view is never obstructed. The adjacent round dining table offers plenty of room for gathering for work or entertainment. Floor-to-ceiling sheer draperies frame each window and, along with the custom-made rug, add a layer of softness to the space.

Photographs by Christopher Luker

"When combining styles, the old and the new, the vintage and contemporary, there is a sweet spot. You have to marry it all up just right so the unexpected feels collected."

–Cindy Meador

ABOVE LEFT: This bathroom feels like you're walking into a spa. The cabinet design with the x-shaped detail on the doors, the subtle frame around the mirror, the Quartzite countertops—it's the perfect place to relax while gazing out at the Gulf of Mexico through the tall window.

ABOVE RIGHT: The dining room is part of the open-concept living and dining space in the beachfront home. Sea glass chairs and a long farm table create a breezy, calming feel that's the perfect combination of contemporary design and cottage warmth. Tall windows provide breathtaking views of the Gulf just steps from the home.

Photographs by Christopher Luker

COLLINS & DUPONT DESIGN GROUP

NAPLES, FL

Innovative and personal, the team at Collins & DuPont Design Group—founded by Kim Collins and Sherri DuPont in 1987—brings stunning designs to life no matter the style. From contemporary to traditional and everything in between, the projects are infinitely individual, representing the team's dedication to building to their clients' unique lifestyles and personalities. Working with Collins & DuPont involves more than just designing beautiful spaces. They know that the process can be very stressful for homeowners. That's why providing a full-service concierge experience is so important—the team wants homeowners to have fun while building their home.

Walk through an Alina Dolan home and you'll find many familiar design elements with a twist. The designer continually looks for new ways to do things, making traditional patterns or design ideas relevant and fresh again. Traditional tapestry patterns may be blown up to create large-scale impact, and industrial elements may be surprisingly juxtaposed with organic pieces to capture the feel of homeowners' dreams. Despite the design group's size, the experience for each homeowner is personal and friendly. That's what brings them back as they move into new homes or their tastes evolve over the years.

LEFT: This home radiates coastal comfort and relaxed elegance. Walking up the grand staircase, one is presented with the breathtaking view of the Gulf through the back pocket doors, which stack into the side walls completely, making the open floorplan even larger, extending onto the outdoor living space. Organic undertones and industrial elements combine to give a cutting edge feel. Layered drop ceiling details over the dining table, the living area, and in the kitchen help delineate the individual spaces within the open plan.
Photograph courtesy of Collins & DuPont Design Group

"You always want to intrigue the eye, but not overwhelm it, with fine details."
—Alina Dolan

ABOVE LEFT: The oversized coastal contemporary kitchen showcases a clean-lined design with light, rustic linear scraped cabinets and Pompeii quartz countertops, while an hourglass shaped backsplash in blue, white and iridescent bronze glass add a touch of vibrancy. Tall display cabinets in a diamond dust Mocha lacquer finish allow for an added touch of height and interest to the space.

ABOVE RIGHT: The same finish is carried into the raised dining storage unit at the wetbar. With custom waterfall side accents embedded with crystals, this unique detail helps define the space between the kitchen and dining spaces and introduces a beautiful change in elevation. By adding an upholstered banquette paired with a dark bronze industrial style dining table, it adds an element of architectural interest and definition of individual spaces. The rustic character, mixed materials, and industrial touches all work in perfect harmony to create this relaxed coastal retreat.

FACING PAGE TOP: The foyer entrance to this 4,917-square-foot home creates an impactful statement by accenting bold checkerboard patterned floors and dark metal details. With large scale rectilinear panel moldings leading from the entry into the stairwell, the space features geometrically undulated balustrades in a dark metal finish and oversized newel posts. All of these features coordinate with the wire brushed oak floors. This area is the perfect start to a home full of harmony and compatibility.

FACING PAGE BOTTOM: The soft contemporary design of this space radiates coastal comfort and relaxed elegance. With the blending of neutral, earth tones and expertly coordinated pops of color and texture, the room is perfectly juxtaposed. Small accent features, like the ceiling detail, create a feeling of openness and fluidity.

Photographs courtesy of Collins & DuPont Design Group

"Take a traditional pattern and blow it up and you've got a fresh, modern take on something that's historically relevant."

—Alina Dolan

ABOVE: The applied panel molding ceiling detail in the master suite was inspired by a traditional pattern that was then blown up and simplified to create a truly unique design that feels familiar. All of the wood elements, including the planked wood headboard wall, were painted in the same tone to create interest without interfering with the fantastic vistas.

FACING PAGE TOP LEFT: The master bathroom features patchwork tiles from Spain. In the shower, a niche set four inches into the wall provides a sleek place for the storage of soap and shampoo bottles. The same tile was used below the soaking tub to mimic a rug.

FACING PAGE TOP RIGHT & FACING PAGE BOTTOM: The upstairs entertainment room sits opposite the master suite and is the epitome of bringing the outdoors in. The room is awash in aqua, grey, and sand tones. The multi-stepped, tri-coffered ceiling adds height to the room, where a mix of industrial, modern, and organic elements mingle to create a warm and welcoming space.

Photographs courtesy of Collins & DuPont Design Group

"Take risks where it makes sense, like in the guest bedroom or with ceiling architecture, to add interest without overwhelming the space."

—Alina Dolan

ABOVE LEFT: A bold intersecting beam ceiling draws the eye in the guest bedroom, where soft washed sage and bright blue combine to create a space that feels exotic and serene. Whimsical elements, like the intertwined metal chair, funky chandelier with exposed bulbs, and cute cat sculpture under the window delight guests who call this space "home."

ABOVE RIGHT: The coordinating bathroom is long but not very wide. Ceilings were kept as high as possible, but were dropped a bit to add intimacy to the space. A long countertop with a hefty front and mitered edge is a dramatic element that also serves to ground the room. Pendant lights flank each mirror, which are a fun mix of the traditional and contemporary.

FACING PAGE TOP: The outdoor living space features tile flooring that matches the hardwood floors in the open living-dining-kitchen area. When the pocket doors are fully opened, the indoor and outdoor living areas appear to be one large space. Multi-level details on the entertainment wall, a large circular dining table, and multiple seating options make it the perfect place for entertaining.

FACING PAGE BOTTOM: The great room features a wall of hexagonal tile in natural slate. When the light hits it just right, it has a subtle metallic sheen. The swirling organic wood sculpture in the corner was crafted from a single piece of wood. Industrial and organic elements, like the cocktail table, which features bolted metal on one side and organic wood on the other, give the room an edge. The wet bar leads to the wine cellar and provides ample storage for glassware and spirits.

Photographs courtesy of Collins & DuPont Design Group

HARRY GANDY HOWLE ARCHITECTS & ASSOC.

VERO BEACH, FL

Harry Howle's work spans the highlands of North Carolina to Florida's coastline and is as far reaching as Cozumel. Holding licensed certification in the allied disciplines of architecture, landscape architecture, and interior design, Harry and his firm competently understand, plan, and provide for every aspect of design. However it really goes beyond that, long before Harry's career began more than three decades ago.

A native of South Carolina's coastal plain, where some of the most splendid examples of Southern Classical domestic architecture exist, Harry absorbed the presence of these structures growing up. His early exposure to the grand style and reasoned order of these distinguished plantation homes imbued him with his intuitive classical approach to architecture. It simply became second nature to him.

Later on, Harry's innate design skills were deftly honed during his education at Clemson University and the University of Georgia. In addition, he has been profoundly influenced by the architectural treatises of Vitruvius and Palladio, who both defined the splendor of classical antiquity, as well as the Spanish Colonial vernacular Addison Mizner brought to Palm Beach in the 1920s. In particular Harry respects Mizner's penchant for blurring the distinction between inside and outside through the generous use of wide balconies, glazed cloister ways and open loggia rooms.

"Classical architecture is not susceptible to casual interpretation because it is based on exacting mathematical proportions."

—Harry G. Howle

ABOVE: This example of Classicism bathed in the glow of the setting sun is an expression of pure classical antiquity employing the Ionic Order. The Orders of classical architecture are not susceptible to casual interpretation because each is composed of a melody of exacting components. The comparative relationships of these Orders from the simplest to the most complex are closely related by a series of mathematical progressions that have stood the test of time.
Photograph by Michael Fuller

FACING PAGE TOP: The Sylvester palms stand as sentries guarding the approach from the lower garden of this residence offering filtered shade around the languid pool and an array of dancing shadows on the surfaces below them.

FACING PAGE BOTTOM LEFT: The kitchen takes its leading role from the movie "Something's Gotta Give" using white antique style cabinetry, stainless commercial appliances, soapstone countertops and white subway tile for the backsplashes.

FACING PAGE BOTTOM RIGHT: A popular feature for an outdoor lifestyle includes areas for alfresco dining, while offering a view of the pool and the placid serenity of the body of water beyond. These living areas are also used to provide a seemingly transparent transition between indoor and outdoor spaces.
Photographs by George Cott

PREVIOUS PAGES: The presence of the portico overlooking the pool is a reflection of the precepts of its chosen vernacular in its purest form, avoiding the pitfalls of eclecticism, which tends to promote architectural contradictions and a lack of discernible style.
Photograph by C. J. Walker

ABOVE: The reasoned order of this beautiful Georgian façade is created by the correct use of its architectural principles resulting in the properly measured proportions to present a welcoming greeting upon arrival to this beachfront residence.

RIGHT: There is always something magical about the serenity of a veranda that evokes memories of lazy summer afternoons curled up on a sofa, book in hand, savoring sweet tea and bathed by the soothing ocean breezes.

FACING PAGE: Upon entering the residence, the stair hall presents a double-helix staircase beautifully crafted with marble treads and decorative iron handrails, which beckons one's ascension to the sanctuary of the private quarters above.

Photographs by Kim Sargent

"Domestic architecture should be a result of the fulfillment of a homeowner's dreams, but it must respect the purest precepts of its chosen vernacular."

—Harry G. Howle

ABOVE: The historical antecedents of the architectural vernacular coined "Anglo-Caribbean," draw a resemblance to 16th-century St. Augustine and other small settlements in the Caribbean islands. These outposts were first settled by the Spanish, building single-story masonry structures along narrow streets. Wood-framed upper stories were added by the English in the 1700s.
Photograph by Robert Brantley

FACING PAGE TOP: Beyond the entry portal of the British West Indies vernacular residence awaits the intrigue of an enchanting courtyard surrounded by columned loggias and the soothing resonance of water dancing in the fountain.
Photograph by Kim Sargent

FACING PAGE BOTTOM: Arriving home, this welcoming feature embellished with mahogany doors and columned pergola greets the owner with space to stow away the classic automobiles, while the Cotswold dormer provides refreshing light to the service quarters above.
Photograph by Kim Sargent

HYATT DESIGN

ORLANDO, FL

Primarily working within the most prestigious residential communities in central Florida, Greg Hyatt designs one-of-a-kind properties that wholly reflect the personal taste of his clients. With more than two decades in the industry, his award-winning firm, Hyatt Design, specializes in making its clients' imagined dream homes become a functionally effective and beautifully designed reality.

Floorplan innovations, efficient space planning techniques, and elevation styles are all specifically customized to the client or builder's needs. No detail is overlooked when it comes to a Hyatt home—from the carefully considered façade of the property to the precise placement of windows to maximize lakefront views and a ceiling design that creates visual interest. Likewise, the transitions between spaces are designed to be graceful and natural, effectively integrating an indoor-outdoor lifestyle.

No two properties are alike with Hyatt Design, as Hyatt seamlessly moves between architectural styles the likes of traditional, contemporary, transitional, French country, and Mediterranean in pursuit of expressing his clients' individuality and manifesting their vision. After all, his motto is that he is not designing a house for his clients; rather, he is designing a home with them.

LEFT: At 12,000 square feet, the Isleworth home is a magnanimous statement property located in a prominent, luxury golf community in central Florida. It reflects the epitome of a true Mediterranean-style aesthetic, with the classic stucco façade, barrel tile roof, and the wrought-iron, castle-front door all creating an intrinsic sense of European-forward romance. An open-plan design takes direct advantage of the views out to the pool and the lake beyond.
Photographs courtesy of Hyatt Design

"Home design is a two-way dialogue between architect and client with each finished property beautifully illustrating this personal conversation."

—Greg Hyatt

ABOVE: Located west of central Florida, the Bella Collina Street of Dreams home is indeed a very sweet Mediterranean dream with the iconic stucco design highlighted by precast stone columns and trim. Built on a very narrow lot with a deep slope, the 8,500-square-foot property maximizes the challenging footprint with a majestic two-story living room that looks directly out onto an infinity edge pool as well as Lake Sienna beyond.

FACING PAGE TOP: Symmetry is key at the Lake Nona home, which is a study in pristine balance and Italianate style. The 7,000-square-foot lakefront property takes full advantage of the Florida lifestyle with exterior spaces that are just as grand and exciting as the interior.

FACING PAGE BOTTOM LEFT: Entertaining is a must with the outdoor lounge and pool, which serves as a proper, open-air extension of the Lake Nona home's indoor family room. The dual-sided fireplace and waterfall, which also houses a TV entertainment system, is just one of the highly customized details of the property.

FACING PAGE BOTTOM RIGHT: This radial staircase, located in the tower of the Bella Collina home, showcases a custom-designed foyer inlay of marble and travertine, which is reflected throughout the house. At the top of the staircase, a statement-making, glass-floored walkway across the living room leads to a wine room.

Photographs courtesy of Hyatt Design

ABOVE & RIGHT: Blending the best of traditional and modern form, the Keenes Point property was custom-built as a Florida vacation home for a client from Brazil. Straight structural lines, flat concrete tile, a contrasting dark roof, and simple windows without articulation or a frame all reflect the transitional style. The interior echoes the striking character of the exterior with such architectural elements as a floating glass staircase and open risers. The house's minimalistic mood makes it a relaxing, low-maintenance place to unwind after the end of a long day of fun.

FACING PAGE TOP: A symmetrical aesthetic was likewise emphasized in this custom property on Lake Butler in Windermere. Designed to capture the essence of the owners' favorite destination, the Bahamas, the Key West-style home features a casually refined, island-influenced aesthetic with grand porches encased with Chippendale railing and details like a hammerhead shark mounted on the wall of the exterior grotto bar. The illuminated functional glass cupola atop the outdoor bar is meant to resemble the shining beacon of a lighthouse.

FACING PAGE BOTTOM: Another example of a Key West-style home in Windermere, this lakeside property celebrates bright, sunny living with a lemony-tinted stucco, a metal roof, and palm trees that only enhance the balanced architectural design.

Photographs courtesy of Hyatt Design

KNIGHT CARR & COMPANY

GREENSBORO, NC

Timeless, classic, refined, relaxed, collected—these are some of the words that illustrate Knight Carr & Company's sophisticated approach to interior direction, where the balance of color, scale, and proportion is paramount. Each project is viewed as a custom one and is considered through multiple dimensions, assuring the final rendition will reflect the lives of the clients with their needs foremost throughout the design process.

"My point of view is to create environments for my clients that speak of fresh yet luxurious style," says owner and designer Linda Knight Carr, who views every project as an artful blend of design, decoration, and collaboration. Together with her innovative and talented team of associates, Linda takes great pride in providing the highest level of service while addressing every last detail.

While the firm is based in North Carolina, the team directs interiors across the United States. Whether it's a casual farmhouse renovation in the Pennsylvania countryside, a corporate office at the nation's capital, a yacht in Charleston harbor, or a beach-side haven in the Florida Keys, Knight Carr & Company delivers uncompromising attention to detail in their statement-making work.

LEFT: With a quietly subtle flair, the formal sitting area in a Charlotte, North Carolina residence softly infuses modern elements into traditional elegance. As the third home that Knight Carr has designed for the client, the space seamlessly integrates pieces from the other properties in combination with updated furnishings and accents. The minimalist lines of the backless sofa and the tall Lucite pedestals contemporize the classic antiques and dark, ebony floors while the simplification of the window treatments effectively incorporates the exterior, further ensuring a light-rich, open aesthetic.
Photograph by Dustin Peck

"My express desire as a designer is to create an environment that speaks the client's language with an expertly directed polish."

—Linda Knight Carr

ABOVE LEFT: Linda Knight Carr cozies up to a cheerful sitting room she designed to be whimsical and delightfully fun. While it's a small space, happiness pervades its entirety thanks to bright pops of pink, a playful mosaic cabinet accented with geometric mirrors, and a paper and Lucite art piece of the image of birds flying through a cotton-candy-hued sky.
Photograph by Scout Guide

ABOVE RIGHT: The side room, located off of a main living salon in a Palm Beach, Florida residence, is all about reflection—literally. Two walls are completely rendered in glass to overlook the waterfront outside while a third mirrored wall replicates the view. Sheer draperies ensure that none of the fresh, light-filled quality is lost. Glossy marble flooring adds even more of a reflective quality.
Photograph by Mark Salisbury

FACING PAGE: A formal yet flexible dining room was in order for a homeowner in Greensboro, North Carolina who entertains frequently. Elegantly upholstered, comfortable chairs with iron bases were designed to seamlessly flow into the living room to create additional space for an open cocktail party setting. A meshing of different periods and patterns adds a layered sense of depth to the space, where the 18th century antique sideboard blends with the delicate edge of a chandelier and the modern curves of the silver nickel and wood dining table. Abstract paintings play off the subtle, woven animal pattern of the chairs and the floral rug.
Photograph by Mark Salisbury

"A space must have soul; it should reflect the lives within. Through this reflection, the space becomes an environment where comfort and beauty thrive."

—Linda Knight Carr

RIGHT: Formal elegance mixes with a more minimalist viewpoint in this entry hall that features a classic velvet chaise longue and printed grass cloth wall covering. The large mirror reflects the Corbin Bronze and the equally sculptural staircase.
Photograph by Dustin Peck

FACING PAGE TOP: Elegantly feminine and full of light, this master suite in a Key West, Florida residence represents the cool breeze of the ocean while celebrating all the natural beauty of its surroundings. The space is formal yet fresh and approachable thanks to a palette in delicate shades of pale blues and warm ivories, which symbolize the water and the sand that's literally footsteps from the bedroom doors leading directly outside to the pool and the beach beyond.
Photograph by Mark Salisbury

FACING PAGE BOTTOM: What's most eye-catching about this vignette is likely the art on the wall above the midcentury wooden cabinet—and that's exactly how it should be. The statement collage by artist Paul Russo was a commissioned work intended to immortalize the homeowner's published cookbook by incorporating every page of it. The green, leafy pattern of the two upholstered side chairs echoes the movement of the collage and its earthy palette of green, sienna, and brown.
Photograph by Mark Salisbury

LAURIE MCRAE INTERIORS

AUGUSTA, GA

Interior design will always be Laurie McRae's first love, but her passion for antiques runs a close second. At Laurie McRae Interiors, both of her passions work hand in hand. With more than 35 years of experience, she continues to set herself apart with a discerning eye that celebrates a classically timeless aesthetic. Her work runs the gamut from residential and commercial projects to hospitality and healthcare design. But she takes special delight in historic homes and renovations where she can pay homage to their heritage while also incorporating modern functionality and serving her clients' individualized needs and tastes.

Laurie not only excels in giving birth to beautiful design, but also in effective project and construction management. She is a licensed interior designer in the state of Georgia and sat on the State Licensing Board of Architects and Interior Designers for seven years. Certified by NCIDQ (National Council for Interior Design Qualification), she has also served on that board and as president. In addition, she also holds the certification for kitchen and bath design (NKBA) and is a certified fine arts appraiser.

Her professional certifications speak to Laurie's expanded knowledge that enhances the function of her spaces and supports universal design, accommodating multiple generations and lifestyles. Likewise, her study and teaching of historical styles also informs her overarching vision and perspective, providing inspiration and depth to her work from every angle.

"The use of quality classics provides a modern yet timeless aesthetic without becoming too trendy."

—Laurie McRae

ABOVE: The blended Asian and American heritage of the homeowners inspired the use of Asian accent pieces throughout the home, including a pair of crane illustrations in the formal dining room. Designed for entertaining, the room can easily seat 10 to accommodate a large and multigenerational extended family.

FACING PAGE: Featuring a modern twist on tradition, the main living areas seamlessly integrate into the home's classic Georgian style, designed by renowned Atlanta architect William T. Baker. A neutral palette of warm gray tones and mixed metals plays beautifully with the transitional furnishings that were specifically selected for their ability to maintain a sense of fresh relevance for years to come.

PREVIOUS PAGES: A full renovation of the kitchen was one of the centerpiece projects of this remodeled, 5,100-square-foot home in the Buckhead area of Atlanta, Georgia. While the original kitchen was well-designed for cooking, the back of the island was an organic, undulating shape that prohibited conversation. By turning it into an L-shape and engineering a quarter-round table top, it became a far more effective space for feeding and withstanding the family's two active boys. The emphasis on clean, modern lines is demonstrated through the linear, water-etched stone and glossy nickel, while an early 20th century sea glass light fixture adds a storied layer to the space.

Photographs courtesy of Steve Bracci Photography

"There is an incredible depth and patina to be gained by incorporating old, antique items into a more contemporary space."

—Laurie McRae

ABOVE: The home's study takes a more lighthearted approach to what can be a traditionally heavy room. Sturdier, masculine furnishings are balanced with the textural edge of thin cork wall covering, gracefully curved lamps, and a quirky white rhinoceros mount that pays homage to the owners' sense of humor. Antique Oriental wall panels add another layer of depth.

FACING PAGE TOP: The master bedroom suite is a peaceful haven where the monochromatic palette still boasts plenty of visual interest. The artwork on the walls was custom-printed to echo the breezy window treatments that feature a tonal tree motif.

FACING PAGE BOTTOM: Accessories boasting bold colors serve to introduce an intentionally bright splash of vibrancy to the serene gray tones of the living room. Yet they can be readily edited and replaced to reflect changing styles or mood. The turquoise urns on the mantel are from the 1930s.

Photographs courtesy of Steve Bracci Photography

MONOGRAM BUILDERS

CLEARWATER, FL

Tim Stroyne long had a dream to create a construction company that was committed to serving clients, architects, and designers at the highest level while building their visions into realities. He founded Monogram Builders in 1994, making that dream a reality. The firm continues to capitalize on Tim's experience and has grown into a talented team of administrators, estimators, managers, superintendents, rough-framing carpenters, finish-trim carpenters, and painters.

Nathan Matthews joined Monogram as chief estimator and quickly became an indispensable member. Nathan's degrees in business administration and construction technology, 20 years of construction experience, and hands-on demeanor make him a perfect business partner, which he became in 2012. "Nate" is also a Certified General Contractor and LEED accredited professional.

Recognized as one of the most respected and successful construction companies in the Tampa Bay area, Monogram is hyper-focused on meeting and exceeding expectations. The firm specializes in both new construction as well as renovations and additions to existing buildings and structures. With high-end residential and commercial projects in Pinellas, Hillsborough, Pasco, Marion and Sarasota counties, Monogram boasts a client list that has grown steadily through the years.

LEFT: A property developer in Tampa Bay turned to Monogram to build his own personal home. While the expansiveness of the 11,840-square-foot coastal home is what catches the eye, its detailed craftsmanship is what holds the gaze. Taking advantage of the intercoastal view, the home celebrates an indoor-outdoor lifestyle with an exterior living area and kitchen that includes a pizza oven along with a negative edge pool, fire pit, and spa.
Photograph courtesy of Monogram Builders

"The highest quality of construction craftsmanship sets the tone for a home, providing a robust platform to build upon."

—Tim Stroyne

ABOVE: The walnut-stained wood floors and walnut cabinets create a welcoming backdrop for this traditional kitchen that was designed to incorporate the views out to the water.

FACING PAGE TOP: Cape Cod-inspired and clad in all-natural cedar shakes, the 11,000-square-foot property brought the charms of traditional Northeastern design to Belleair, Florida.

FACING PAGE BOTTOM LEFT: Located on the exterior of the front of the home, the rotunda serves as a sitting area for the master suite and provides beautiful waterside views. Aside from the view, the structure itself makes a statement with its artfully carved ceiling and rounded crown molding.

FACING PAGE BOTTOM RIGHT: The home's rich, sturdy architectural aesthetic is readily demonstrated in the family room, where the recessed ceiling and solid wood beams make a statement from the start—and also seamlessly disguise the duct work.

Photographs courtesy of Monogram Builders

"A mix of construction materials not only creates interesting visual texture, it softens the barrier between the interior and the exterior."

—Tim Stroyne

ABOVE LEFT: The foyer is an enlightening welcome to the home, where the two-story ceiling provides a sense of light openness. The rugged, stone-clad walls flow seemlessly between the inside and outside.

ABOVE RIGHT: The living room's unusual vaulted ceiling draws the eye upward while a sleek, horizontally oriented fireplace detail grounds the space as does the lower profile of the furnishings. The repetition of the stained wood creates continuity.

FACING PAGE TOP: Positioned at the furthest west point of Culbreath Isles, the contemporary stunner was built on a cul de sac and boasts one of the best views of Tampa Bay, Florida. While modern in design, the front elevation of the home also shows its prairie-style influences with the low-pitched roof and amplified overhangs.

FACING PAGE BOTTOM: The expansive outdoor living area capitalizes on the encompassing panoramic view. The space echoes the mix of materials used inside with the repetition of stained cypress ceilings and cultured stone.

Photographs courtesy of Monogram Builders

"Elegance is captured in the integrity of even the smallest, most unexpected detail."

—Tim Stroyne

TOP: The foyer is formally elegant, punctuated by a grand staircase and custom railing, with walls clad in tonal wainscoting.

MIDDLE: While the pool table and circular bar in the game room get top billing, the knotty alder wood ceiling shares center stage with its impressive level of design. Its picture frame, tongue-in-groove design is only matched by the wagon-wheel detail that reflects the shape of the bar.

BOTTOM: The expansive kitchen, which was configured to look out to the pool, is a cook's dream with three islands and a breakfast area. The space, which also leads into the family room, keeps a fresh perspective with cabinets painted in a creamy, latte finish.

FACING PAGE TOP: Inspired by French sophistication, this Belleair, Florida property was completed for the homeowner in a comparatively short 20 months. Yet, no detail was spared with the highest quality of materials implemented in the design. The all-natural stone exterior, pre-cast concrete columns, and slate roof all contribute to the grandeur of the home.

FACING PAGE BOTTOM: Covering approximately 8,000 square feet, the large pool and outdoor deck and dining pavilion serve to also visually unite the main house to the guest house.

Photographs courtesy of Monogram Builders

NEAL PRINCE STUDIO

GREENVILLE, SC

Neal Prince Studio, the custom residential design studio of LS3P, prides itself in exceeding its clients' goals through thoughtful, innovative, and timeless designs. Established in 1969 by architect Jim Neal, the studio is founded upon Neal's belief that each client is unique, and that everyone deserves to live in a well-designed home. The design process begins with listening, and the design team is passionate about tailoring each home to the individual needs of those who will live there.

Neal Prince Studio works at all scales, from small renovations to luxury resort homes, and recognizes that great design is not restricted to a particular housing type, size, or style. The studio is highly experienced in designs for new homes, urban infill sites, additions, historic renovations, and affordable workforce housing. Since long before the current green revolution, sustainable design has been a guiding principle for the team; more than four decades of design excellence have demonstrated that energy efficient, ecologically sensitive designs go hand-in-hand with beauty and function.

Neal Prince Studio has mastered the art of offering small-firm client relationships with large-firm resources, yielding the studio an award-winning portfolio of projects across the Southeast and beyond.

Justin

ABOVE & RIGHT: With the northern waters of Lake Keowee as the backdrop, the home at Paw Paw Point provides an ideal retreat from everyday life. This home is set on a scenic peninsula at Keowee Vineyards and uses indigenous natural elements like fieldstone and cedar to create the simple comfort and laid-back feel that the homeowners wanted. Every room offers sweeping views of the waterfront, providing a sense of serenity throughout the home.
Photograph by Firewater Photography

FACING PAGE: When designing this home at Top Ridge Drive, the clients' passion for entertaining was a priority. The layout of the shingle-style home offers a casual atmosphere so guests feel relaxed and comfortable, even though the home is a generous 8,900 square feet. At ground level, the homeowners have everything they need for gatherings and parties—the kitchen, dining, media, and great rooms—while the upper level allows for private spaces like the master suite and guest rooms to remain secluded. A distinctive octagonal tower provides an observatory for experiencing the full breadth of the surrounding lake views.
Photograph by Taylor Architectural Photography

PREVIOUS PAGES: This home at the Cliffs of Glassy Mountain takes full advantage of spectacular views. A linear plan features 18-foot-tall windows that create a transparent wall, allowing clear sight lines across the impressive valley and lake below. The three-story, 5,100-square-foot residence appears to be an extension of the rocky terrain and utilizes a warm palette of fieldstone, river rock, Brazilian cherry floors, and cedar trellises to preserve its natural feel.
Photograph by Taylor Architectural Photography

PEPE CALDERIN DESIGN

MIAMI, FL

Fresh, dynamic, and visionary are just a few of the words used to describe Pepe Calderin Design's body of work that spans four continents and has earned national and international design accolades for its variety of spaces and styles. With more than 20 years of experience, the Florida- and New York-based modern interior design firm creates high-end residential and commercial spaces that are strongly saturated with energy and warmth.

The company's namesake founder and principal, Pepe Calderin, prizes nothing more than finding beauty in the everyday and making it extraordinary. He and his firm offer a full range of design services including concept and space planning, construction and permit consulting, and three-dimensional renderings, along with purchasing and installation for materials, furniture, and lighting.

However, it is the remarkably collaborative service that is at the heart of Pepe Calderin Design's mission. Every one of the firm's projects invariably becomes a distinctive and dynamic reflection of the respective client's unique personality, lifestyle, and spirit.

LEFT: A statement-making showpiece perched 50 stories in the air, the Akoya penthouse in Miami Beach, Florida is a modern marvel that takes full advantage of endless ocean views with the rooftop terrace that blurs the line between interior and exterior. An infinity pool and Jacuzzi, situated atop a raised wood deck, along with an outdoor kitchen and lounge area, not to mention the building's striking, triangular architecture all make for quite the glorious destination for entertaining or relaxation.
Photographs courtesy of Pepe Calderin Design

ABOVE: At 6,000 square feet, the Akoya penthouse was fully gutted to transform the building developer's standard, compartmentalized layout to a more contemporary, light-filled space. The owners, who use the apartment as a getaway from their house in the city, wanted a highly unique, modern aesthetic that was still warm and inviting. Natural woods, translucent glass and onyx, and an innovative indoor water feature echo the exterior surroundings and balance the sleek coolness of the furniture and fixtures. The seating arrangements were designed to maximize the spectacular ocean views—yet again bridging the outside with the inside.
Photographs courtesy of Pepe Calderin Design

FACING PAGE TOP: Refinement and warmth in combination with a sense of bold playfulness dominate the private residence in Miami Beach, Florida. Once a small, three-bedroom house, the property was transformed into a luxurious, five-bedroom estate with an open, spacious layout. The modern aesthetic is immediately recognizable in the main living area, where a neutral, elegant background of soft tones, warm woods, and an onyx fireplace only further provide the canvas for bright, graphic artwork, colorful accent furniture pieces, and an eye-catching linear rug.

FACING PAGE BOTTOM: The classic yet youthfully exuberant spirit continues in this lounge space in the Doral Residence, where the rich use of red accents against a cool palette of white and charcoal gray provides a sense of design continuity. Window treatments were kept sheer and light to allow hazy glimpses to the ocean outside even when fully closed.

"Interior design is much like storytelling; it has the power to evoke a compelling sense of emotion when an artful balance of elements are woven together."

—Pepe Calderin

ABOVE LEFT: Modern, sleek elegance begins in the penthouse's foyer with the soft color story of white, gray, and lavender mixed with glossy marble and shiny metals.

ABOVE RIGHT: The grandeur of the living area is reflected even more in the striking wall of horizontal mirrors that creates more depth and drama within the room.

FACING PAGE: A once-traditional, 7,000-square-foot penthouse in Hollywood, Florida, received a contemporary makeover and a new lease on life after a two-year remodeling project that transformed the space into the dream home for a retired couple. The living room's 20-foot, floor-to-ceiling windows do a splendid job of showcasing the oceanfront views while providing plenty of natural light throughout the day. The second floor of the unit creates a lower ceiling for the living area's adjacent dining room, where a dark statement wall creates a mood of distinction and a large, custom-designed glass-topped dining table ensures a sense of openness remains intact.

Photographs courtesy of Pepe Calderin Design

"A space has no boundaries and has endless possibilities."

—Pepe Calderin

ABOVE LEFT: The owners of the 3,500-square-foot New York City residence had two things in mind when it came to the redesign of their home: form and function. Not only was stylish modernity top of mind so, too, was practical kid-friendliness for their growing family. The open layout of the main living area is not only perfect for entertaining, the soft and sophisticated textiles are durable and stain-resistant. An octagonal dining table creates a strong focal point while also separating the living room from the family room.

ABOVE RIGHT: The New York City residence's neutral color scheme is emboldened by gold, black, and lilac accents along with abstract patterns, echoed in both the art and the rug, that emphasize movement. The original floors were stained in a dark tobacco finish for a rich contrast to the rest of the lighter palette. The open plan also directly guides the eye to the spectacular city views outside.

FACING PAGE: From the moment the doors open to the front entry, there is a flair for the dramatic. The combination of antique glass with an oversized round mirror along with a gold-leaf sideboard and onyx and glass drops chandelier sets the mood for the luxurious elegance and warmth that's to follow in the rest of the home.

Photographs courtesy of Pepe Calderin Design

PUSCHENDORF INTERIORS

MIAMI, FL

Each space has something special just waiting to be revealed through design. Aldo Puschendorf, principal of Puschendorf Interiors, believes that a room can be truly appreciated through its complementary décor. Crisp, clean lines, minimal color, and zero clutter are hallmarks of Aldo's work, but it is his clients who truly inspire him. Whether their style is preppy, artistic, or sophisticated, homeowners appreciate how well Aldo captures their personalities through unique designs.

Aldo hails from a rich cultural background, having been born in Latin America and raised in southern Louisiana—where he attended the University of New Orleans and Tulane University for architecture design—before moving to South Florida in 1995. That diversity helps inform his design style, which is flexible and complementary to his clients' needs, while always maintaining a fresh aesthetic that's equally modern and warm. From full-scale interior design to creating custom furniture, upholstery, and kitchens, Aldo and his team pride themselves on giving homeowners a turnkey experience. Working with a team of licensed architects and general contractors, Puschendorf Interiors places the client first and is prepared to lead them through every step of the design process, from the structure itself to the finishing touches.

LEFT: Upon exiting the elevator, one enters the condo via the foyer, featuring marble floors, and stunning sycamore panels and doors with custom hardware. The sculptural chair in the foyer causes one to pause before passing through to the entryway with its matching sycamore wall panels. The console table, a Puschendorf design, features antiques from the Ming Dynasty.
Photograph courtesy of Puschendorf Interiors

"Clean lines and minimal colors help you to appreciate all the space and its views have to offer."

—Aldo Puschendorf

ABOVE: The beachy, contemporary home in Boca Raton, right by the water, is airy and peaceful. Each piece of furniture was designed and built specifically for the space, which is not overly accessorized. Grey-beige porcelain planks ground the room, while touches of yellow add a pop of color to the otherwise monochromatic palette.

FACING PAGE TOP: Custom sofas sit across from one another with a Puschendorf-designed coffee table between them. The ceilings in the home were dropped about three inches to conceal the mechanisms for the shades and wires for lighting. Accent lighting highlights the spherical artwork on the back wall, while mesh Calvin Klein draperies add a fluid quality to the space—their sheen and shimmer make them appear to be moving.

FACING PAGE BOTTOM: "His den" features a table of Aldo's own design, a custom sofa, and custom chairs already owned by the homeowners. Impressive views serve as a beautiful backdrop for the room. Beyond the den arrangement, the breakfast area capitalizes on these views and sits adjacent to the kitchen.

Photographs courtesy of Puschendorf Interiors

"Design is the expression of the owners' personalities, lives, and tastes."
—Aldo Puschendorf

ABOVE: The Boca Raton kitchen features grey cabinets with white quartz countertops. The long bar ends with a custom dining table, offering ample seating for friends and family. White painted glass doors conceal pantries at both ends of the kitchen, adding yet another contemporary element to the room.

FACING PAGE TOP: Feminine touches make "her den" a place for relaxation and entertaining. A vintage 1950s chair joins a custom-made sofa bed. Clean lines and subtle colors allow the artwork to take center stage in the room.

FACING PAGE BOTTOM LEFT: Aldo designed every piece in the room, which features three enclaves in the wall for added interest. The soothing space benefits from a pop of red.

FACING PAGE BOTTOM RIGHT: The classic contemporary home features all plaster walls, marble floors, clean lines, and easy elegance.
Photographs courtesy of Puschendorf Interiors

READER & SWARTZ ARCHITECTS

WINCHESTER, VA

The open exchange of ideas serves as the cornerstone of every project at Reader & Swartz Architects. Founded by Beth Reader, FAIA, and Chuck Swartz, AIA, this architecture firm, nestled in the Shenandoah Valley of Virginia, encourages a collaborative design process that helps its team navigate project design and construction. Their commitment to this philosophy of collaboration can even be seen visually in their open studio workspace.

The key to their success is developing a design concept that resonates with the client, as well as the site. They purposely steer away from specializing in one style, as the lack of specialization encourages questioning and listening. By talking extensively with clients and thoroughly studying the site with them, the team at Reader & Swartz helps clients make educated decisions that result in houses that honor their places and are wonderful to be in. Throughout the design process, the clients and the builders remain engaged, allowing the firm to create timeless and imaginative solutions.

LEFT: There were several major drivers in the design of the vacation home on the banks of the Shenandoah River. The owner, a New York City resident, wanted to escape the hectic lifestyle of the city and have a gathering place for his extended family. It was also important for the house to incorporate a view of, and access to, the river.
Photograph by Nathan Webb, AIA

FACING PAGE TOP: A wall of expansive windows offers river views, as it blurs the line between the home's interior and exterior. Exposed trusses continue the rustic feel, while a cracked glass floor, complete with blue LED lights, pours natural light into the basement hallway during the day and serves as a cosmic nightlight when it's dark.

FACING PAGE BOTTOM: The home celebrates the Shenandoah River, which can be seen and experienced from many angles. In the library, stacked stone tile and wood floors continue the strong connection of the structure to its natural environment.

ABOVE: Built in Shenandoah County, Virginia, the full-time residence offers views of the Shenandoah Valley edged with the Blue Ridge Mountains. The owner, a former Washington, DC-area resident, says, "Weather used to be something I watched on television. Now weather is my television."

RIGHT: Warm, textual materials enrich the home's interior. The large kitchen has a banquette alcove lined with poplar tree bark shingles, and the main dining space features a wood ceiling and a custom light fixture.

Photographs by Nathan Webb, AIA

"We use the site's environment, history, and culture as a starting point for design. History and place help fuel the twin design tools of abstraction and narration, which are used to create buildings that resonate."
—Chuck Swartz

LEFT: A large addition, with a modern take on the historical vernacular architecture, breathed new life into a mid-1800s farmhouse. The renovation and addition to the existing structure provided a platform to explore both the form and function of a modern farmhouse, while offering stunning views of the surrounding landscape.
Photographs by Nathan Webb, AIA

"By listening to clients and working with them and the builder throughout the design process, we create structures that not only celebrate people's lives, but also honor where they are located."

—Chuck Swartz

ABOVE: A combination of traditional, mullioned windows, along with large, open sheets of glass, frame the views of the landscape that surrounds the updated farmhouse. The new kitchen and living wing of the home—with the master suite directly above—open up to the mountain views.

FACING PAGE: The addition's exterior materials, including lap siding in alternating width exposures and galvanized pressed metal, were carefully chosen to express and reinterpret the rural vernacular of the historic home.

Photographs by Nathan Webb, AIA

STAN TOPOL & ASSOCIATES

ATLANTA, GA

Interior designer Stan Topol spent the early summers of his career in a way that most could only dream; he assisted the late Billy Baldwin, who has been called the "dean of American interior decorators," in New York City. Billy's taste and sense of elegance had a profound influence on Stan's own design voice, especially when he established his namesake firm in the mid-1970s. And, ever since, Stan Topol & Associates has been dedicated to the art form of decorating as a way to make life more beautiful while upholding the integrity of good, functional design.

For the award-winning firm, every project begins at the drafting board, where studies and sketches of interior spaces illustrate elements including proportion, space, and furnishings. The clients' needs and personal style are at the forefront, always with a careful eye towards the appropriateness of the décor for the specific room and its architecture. Stan and his team take great pride in listening to each client and educating them on everything from furniture to fabrics, finishes, cabinetry, and art. "We draw from our client's dreams and their requirements as we create a concept of how we can make those thoughts a reality," says Stan.

In addition to the details taken into account for each space including traffic flow, convenience, and interior views, Stan Topol & Associates also has the capacity to produce complete interior construction documents for floor plans, demolition plans, electrical, elevations, and timelines. It all serves to support the firm's distinctive aesthetic and signature work that is never short on the true sense of style—a style built on the foundation of fine arts and not just drafting.

"Great rooms are built and furnished around the people who live in them."

—Stan Topol

ABOVE LEFT: At the end of a long hallway lined with paintings, an understated sitting area is the epitome of cool, calm, and collected elegance. The curvaceous identity of the space reflects the arch of the window and ceilings, with John Boone furnishings circling the delicate edge of the Cedric Hartman centerpiece table.

ABOVE RIGHT: The same curved motif is repeated with the home's remarkable staircase and custom railing that undulates through three floors. The quiet simplicity of the single bench speaks volumes when punctuated by the flush of a Jules Olitsky abstract painting as the vibrant exclamation point to round out the minimal space.

FACING PAGE: A master bathroom becomes experiential art when the shower and tub unite as one, creating a beautifully streamlined effect that's also quite safe and accessible. The gleaming, silver bench adds a sculptural component to the clean, minimal lines.

PREVIOUS PAGES: The beauty and ease of indoor-outdoor living was paramount for this waterfront home in Florida. The expansive veranda is an exterior continuation of the family room, which opens directly onto it. The arrangement of both the sitting and dining areas was designed for conversation and to reflect casual island charm with David Sutherland furnishings including comfortable teak wood chairs, communal tables, and a wood-paneled ceiling accented with the richness of dark, weighty beams. The mirror above the grand, molded fireplace serves a dual purpose, also disguising a television.

Photographs courtesy of Stan Topol & Associates

"We personalize each design concept as we draw from the inside out; we draw the way people actually live."

—Stan Topol

ABOVE & FACING PAGE: Sumptuous refinement is graciously celebrated at this Park Avenue apartment, where the living room is a discreet mix of traditional Regency pieces and contemporary references. The focal point above the J. Robert Scott sofa is a painting by New York City artist Christopher Gallego, which adds a sense of reflective texture. The elegance continues in the master suite, where the statement piece is the custom-designed Rose Tarlow bed, which is bordered in faux ivory. Wall-to-wall window treatments lend a soft grace to the room while also blocking out the sun's rays.

Photographs courtesy of Stan Topol & Associates

"Decoration needs to make life more beautiful without compromising the instinctual essence of style and function."

—Stan Topol

TOP: A bookcase's purpose is regally redefined with the addition of a mirror and a custom, built-in banquette, creating a cozy seating nook in the music room of this Atlanta residence.

BOTTOM: The home's family room was designed for comfort—from the plush J. Robert Scott sofa and side chairs to the upholstered coffee table. Yet it still boasts an uncompromising level of sophistication in the refined fabrics and finishes. The mirrored alcove adds a sense of depth to the room, with its ledge providing a display case of sorts for objets d'art and a Todd Murphy drawing.

FACING PAGE: The living room has a flair for the dramatic in its sharp black-and-white color palette that's enlivened by the strength of a zebra print motif yet simultaneously softened by upholstered walls and a plush sectional, flanked by Rose Tarlow accent pieces. The mix of a classic painting with abstract art that echoes the zebra contributes another layer of intriguing power to the space.

Photographs courtesy of Stan Topol & Associates

WILLIAM ANDREWS ARCHITECTS

KNOXVILLE, TN

Designing with site location, orientation, natural light, and the surrounding environment in mind elevates a home from ordinary to extraordinary. That's what Bill Andrews, principal of William Andrews Architects, does with every design. Bill devotedly maintains his firm's client-driven focus. His clients appreciate the wonderful relationships they develop with Bill and his team, as well as Bill's down-to-earth approach to design–returning time and again as their lives change.

With nearly three decades of experience dedicated exclusively to custom residential architecture and landscape design, Bill's work appears from the Hamptons to Hilton Head. His residential designs have been featured in publications and have earned national awards, including BALA's coveted "Best One-of-a Kind" Custom Home. He is honored that six of his homes have been selected to be on the Knoxville Museum of Art Holiday Home Tour and another featured by the Knoxville Symphony Orchestra as their showcase home. Whether designing a contemporary or traditional home, Bill approaches each project with the same degree of passion and purpose: to create a home that honors the site and serves the owners in a way that resonates with their lives. The result is a home that is both functional and beautiful.

LEFT: West Tennessee limestone turned on opposite sides gives an Old World feel to the home that is a blend between English Tudor and Old English styles. Designed to look more timeless than trendy, the home is a charming combination of artistry and craftsmanship.
Photograph courtesy of William Andrews Architects

"Timeless design has a universal appeal that lasts."

—Bill Andrews

ABOVE: The shingle-style home utilizes a post and beam interior structural system, and the timber frame inside is absolutely breathtaking. The overall design was carried into the backyard, where the pool and landscape continue the organic feel of the home.

FACING PAGE TOP & BOTTOM: The shingle-style home with accents of West Tennessee limestone is the perfect marriage of the house with its site. Built on a hill and complete with a basement, it fits in beautifully with the surrounding landscape.

Photographs courtesy of William Andrews Architects

"Focus on the site and how the home integrates into it for a cohesive look and feel."

—Bill Andrews

TOP LEFT: The design for this cottage on the water employs visual sleight-of-hand, appearing smaller than its actual size. High windows and shingle siding were used to fulfill the owner's desire for a home with the relaxed charm of a rustic fish camp.

MIDDLE LEFT: The back porch features exposed rough-sawn rafters, stone flooring, and a large 12-foot ceiling fan over the seating area.

BOTTOM LEFT: Enhancing the home's old-fashioned rustic feel, the interior walls are clad in lightly sanded horizontal shiplap wood paneling. Natural light floods the space and a large stone fireplace offers a touch of warmth throughout the year.

FACING PAGE TOP & BOTTOM: The shingle-style home features West Tennessee limestone, beautiful white windows, and multiple fireplaces. Designed to look like a North Carolina lodge, the home also boasts a copper roof and a basement.

Photographs courtesy of William Andrews Architects

"Design is not just what it looks like...
design is how it works."
—Steve Jobs

Rona Landman Interior Design , page 161

CHAPTER TWO

Birdseye Design, page 149

Linda Ruderman Interiors, page 157

Northeast

ANTHONY MINICHETTI ARCHITECT

GREENWICH, CT

Anthony Minichetti Architect LLC specializes in luxury residential, resort, and retail environments. An artist at heart, Anthony Minichetti founded his practice after earning a Bachelor of Architecture from The Irwin S. Chanin School of Architecture at The Cooper Union, an elite institution located at Cooper Square in New York City. In addition, he has studied fine art abroad through programs provided by The Cooper Union and The Yale School of Art.

With a strong artistic sensibility, Anthony blends classic architecture with contemporary insight and technique to ensure that his firm's creations, modern or traditional, are timeless in style. A key factor in his design process is collaboration. By carefully listening to the visual imagery clients describe, Anthony creates couture spaces that complement their lifestyles and correctly reflect their personal style. The result is impeccable design that surprises and delights as it effortlessly encourages those who dwell in it to live life to the fullest.

LEFT: A Long Island family who summered in Nantucket annually wanted to bring the architectural flavor of their summer vacations home. In response, Anthony and his team created a contemporary version of Nantucket's architectural style, complete with a front veranda appointed with rocking chairs. Larger scale windows in addition to simplified railing and lattice detailing create a welcome environment punctuated with a pineapple atop the entry portico.
Photograph by Tim Williams

"We attempt to change the design world one project at a time and believe that everyone is entitled to buildings and spaces that support their activity, inspire their actions, and delight their senses."

—Anthony Minichetti

ABOVE: A Long Island beach house offers a contemporary take on the traditional shingle-style home found in coastal regions. Outdoor terraces front every guest suite and a circulation tower appointed with glass walls maximizes breathtaking views of the sea. An invisible-edge pool further heightens the connection of the site to the ocean. The Chippendale fretwork, railings and the bracket detailing were streamlined to create a current look for a young, growing family.
Photograph by Anthony Minichetti

FACING PAGE TOP & BOTTOM LEFT: An oceanfront respite in Key Largo, Florida, exudes an open-air contemporary Bali feel. Lush landscaping complete with meandering paths provides serenity, as the combination perfectly complements the sprawling nature of the structure. With its floating roofline and aqua sea blue accents, the architecture seamlessly blends with the ocean and the skies above creating a magical oasis.
Photographs by Tim Williams

FACING PAGE BOTTOM RIGHT: A secret garden punctuated by a statue of Buddha gives the space the feeling of an abandoned fountain. The home and guesthouse circulate around the secret garden court, providing an intimate setting for entertaining, relaxation and indoor-outdoor living.
Photograph by Tim Williams

BEN KRUPINSKI BUILDER

EAST HAMPTON, NY

Intuitive and precise, Ben Krupinski, principal of Ben Krupinski Builder, possesses an innate understanding of the terrain and the people of his native East Hampton, New York, where many of his stately designs grace lush landscapes. Perhaps unsurprisingly, with this intuitive understanding, he built his first home: his personal residence. Carrying out all the tasks himself—including digging the hole and pouring the concrete for the foundation—Ben discovered his passion for home building. Along with some help from his wife Bonnie, he found that building homes allowed him to spend his days outside and gave him the satisfaction of working with his hands. Early in his career, Ben easily mingled with many people in the homebuilding industry while working for his wife's sand and gravel company. A request from one such acquaintance to install a window provided the impetus to start his business in 1980.

Today his firm is one of the go-to building companies in the Hamptons, and Ben himself is easily recognizable there. A perfectionist and an extremely hard worker, Ben is known for his attention to detail and superior communication with homeowners. Never one to sit in an office, Ben can frequently be found working onsite alongside his craftsmen from start to finish. His clients recognize the passion that flows into each of Ben's projects and value him for his easy, down-to-earth communication style and rigorous design standards. Clients become friends, and Ben is dedicated to caring for homeowners and their homes well after the project is complete.

"The mark of a great builder is they can build anything from traditional to ultramodern, and everything in between, merging classical design with modern sensibilities."

—Ben Krupinski

ABOVE LEFT, ABOVE RIGHT, FACING PAGE & PREVIOUS PAGES: Strong traditional and classic lines dominate the home. Eight stately chimneys dot the roof, while oversized windows flood the interior with clean, bright air.
Photographs by Jeff Heatley

ABOVE: With ocean views, the back of this East Hampton home includes covered patios and a graceful pool.

FACING PAGE TOP LEFT & TOP RIGHT: While a very modern structure, the house sits in perfect harmony with the farmland site. Interesting innovations abound, such as a durable fiberglass roof and a 200-foot wall that provides privacy and acts as an interior wall for portions of the home while functioning as an impressive design element.

FACING PAGE BOTTOM LEFT & BOTTOM RIGHT: The modern staircase with a glass balustrade allows for uninterrupted views out two stories of windows.
Photographs by Thomas Choi

"There's a kind of sixth sense that you develop when you've been somewhere for a long time. You intuitively know what's going to work best with the land."

—Ben Krupinski

ABOVE: A large traditional family home fits seamlessly into the Sagaponack landscape. The warm, comfortable house—an elegant mix of stone, shingling, and wood—shows off an exquisite level of detail inside and out.

FACING PAGE TOP & BOTTOM: Built in record time, the classic Greek revival oceanfront home boasts extensive wooden elements and great public spaces. Warm interiors and staggering views provide a superb atmosphere to entertain.
Photographs by Jeff Heatley

"Great houses are the result of perfectionism at every step of the design and construction process."

—Ben Krupinski

ABOVE, FACING PAGE TOP & BOTTOM: A custom stainless steel elliptical staircase with walnut stair treads, balusters, and custom turned handrails creates a focal point in the full renovation of the pre-war residence that combined two New York City apartments into one striking Manhattan abode. Custom millwork throughout the kitchen pairs with soapstone counters and hand-cut mosaic marble backsplashes.

Photographs courtesy of Ben Krupinski Builders

BETH ANN KESSLER DESIGNS

PHILADELPHIA, PA

For interior designer Beth Ann Kessler, it is the littlest details that make the biggest difference in a space. Since launching her company, Beth Ann Kessler Designs, in 1981, she has paid passionate attention to each of her commercial and residential projects. It's a skill honed by her architecture degree from the University of Michigan and from 25 years of study at The Barnes Foundation, which houses one of the world's finest collections of post-impressionist and early modern paintings.

Kessler's architecture and art background has a profound impact on her aesthetics. It gives her the tools to solve the puzzles of spatial relations and floorplans as well as the ability to manipulate color, light, line, and space. She starts her work with the form (the existing structure), adds the function (what the client needs), and then adds the qualities the client desires. Such impact is readily seen in each of her projects, where her architectural design, space planning, and interior design work in harmony to create a uniquely customized end result.

LEFT: The move from a single-family home to a condominium in suburban Philadelphia necessitated a reconfiguration of existing furniture for a new living room. All the architectural details, wood floor, custom cabinets, and millwork were added. Although the space may not appear contemporary, it actually is a high-tech, smart home with either touch panels or keypads in each room controlling lighting, shades, security, HVAC, music, and more.
Photograph by Halkin Mason Photography

"The difference between what a fine artist does and what I do as a designer is that my work has to be functional."

—Beth Ann Kessler

ABOVE: What once housed an open-plan kitchen was transformed into a dining room. A curved wall with bi-folding passageway doors terminating into recessed pockets was added to create a more formalized separation from the living room. Instead of wallpaper, the blue faux finish creates a textural effect—and a backdrop for art including antique Asian paintings, a still life by Barnes protégé Biagio Pinto and another by realist Willem Dolphyn.

FACING PAGE TOP: A unique feature of the living room and dining room is this custom-designed wall, which is nothing short of an engineering marvel. Each set of doors was carefully constructed to bi-fold into the recessed pockets on the sides of the display case—no small feat, considering its curved shape. Art Deco-inspired, hand-carved flowers form an intricate frame while the same floral shape is echoed in the case's cabinet knobs. The lighting on each glass shelf moves with the shelf when it's repositioned.

FACING PAGE BOTTOM: Additional attention was given to the doors by using ribbon-striped sapele veneer to create a horizontal and vertical block pattern.

Photographs by Halkin Mason Photography

ABOVE: A newly created media room borrowed space from the original living room. Truly a "home-y" theater, it is lined with acoustic panels and has speakers behind the large screen and recessed into the ceiling for superior sound. But the theater isn't just a technical achievement; it raises the bar on design craftsmanship, too. Custom amboyna wood cabinets feature faux ivory inlay of diamond shapes for a subtle Art Deco flair along with an ivory-hued band of fluting that echoes a similar motif in the living room's millwork. The "improved painting" is by surrealistic painter Mati Klarwein, best known for his images on album covers.

RIGHT: The home theater also has a clever addition in its use of a secret door. One of the panels opens to the master bedroom, thus utilizing the home theater as a sitting room for this bedroom while still maintaining privacy between the two spaces when the homeowner is entertaining guests.

FACING PAGE TOP: French glass doors leading to balconettes that line the west side of the living room posed a problem for afternoon sunlight. Custom fabric was selected to use for motorized solar shades since stock material had a moiré, psychedelic effect against the doors' screens. The carved, built-in wood cabinet, centered on the window wall, is the epitome of form and function; it not only conceals a large structural column, but also reveals a thin, large-screen television when the horizontal wood panel slides up. Storage cabinets are located on both sides.

FACING PAGE BOTTOM: To make the non-ducted gas fireplace more aesthetically pleasing, Beth Ann floated it off the floor and surrounded it with travertine marble slab. Floating lacquered shelves mirror the floating fireplace and were added for display. The painting above the mantel is a self-portrait by cubist painter Maria Blanchard. The starburst motif, seen here on the two custom-leaded glass doors that lead into the kitchen, is repeated on wood doors throughout the condo. To the left of the doors is a period cabinet by Art Nouveau practitioner Maurice Dufrene.

Photographs by Halkin Mason Photography

"It's the details that make the difference."

—Beth Ann Kessler

ABOVE: Symmetry creates a sense of peaceful elegance in the master suite. Prominent in this space are the floor-to-ceiling, fluted maple cabinets flanking the television. The built-in cabinet on the right conceals another structural column and still maintains useable, shallow storage behind the doors. Balance is achieved on the left with the addition of a "true" cabinet that allows for storage, including two refrigerator drawers that are convenient for chilled beverages. The soft-pink, moiré faux-painted door is the secret door from the bedroom side that leads into the home theater. The door on the opposite side of the room is the main access to the condo from the bedroom and repeats the starburst pattern.

TOP RIGHT: Beth Ann Kessler perches behind two original Jules Leleu Art Deco chairs, which she had reupholstered in a custom, floral-embossed leather.

BOTTOM RIGHT: The vanity is one of the highlights of the master bathroom. Lalique crystal turns faucet knobs into objects of beauty. The frosted glass continues with the sinks that feature etched flowers and are lit from underneath for a glowing effect. This same flower design is repeated in silver-leafed woodcarvings in the corners of the white lacquered vanity cabinet doors below. Separating the marble countertop from the cabinet doors is the same fluting seen in the living room and in the home theater—only here it is done in silver leaf.

FACING PAGE TOP: The 3-way mirrors in the master bathroom serve double duty as medicine cabinet doors that were purposefully hung 14 inches above the countertop to accommodate bathroom products. The white door with stainless steel inlay was imported from Italy and is designed without a door jam to be flush with the marble walls.

FACING PAGE BOTTOM: The master bathroom is big by most standards at 27 feet x 14 feet. It features his-and-her showers, toilets, and sinks divided by a bathtub and linen closet. Waterproof screens allow for television viewing from the tub as well as from almost any vantage point in the bathroom.

Photographs by Halkin Mason Photography

"Art and life are inseparable. All the qualities that give art its value and make it meaningful are those that are found in everyday life."

—Beth Ann Kessler

ABOVE: The kitchen was relocated to the former den area of the home to accomplish two main goals: first, it was to be closed off from the main living area; and second, it was to have access to natural light, which was missing in the original kitchen space. White lacquer cabinetry, quartz countertops, porcelain floors, and stainless steel appliances are glossy yet durable.

FACING PAGE TOP: The foyer sets the tone for the condo with its eclectic mix of contemporary and traditional design. The gold-leaf wallpaper that covers the ceiling delivers a reflective quality that's echoed in the illuminated curved wall showcasing a bronze sculpture by Argentine artist Marta Minujin. Perhaps the most intriguing ensemble in the entry features a white tufted leather sofa by famed Spanish designer Jaime Hayden along with a pair of Baccarat sconces and an Andy Warhol screenprint, "Macintosh." The art not only speaks to the homeowner's love of the Apple brand, but is also a cheeky nod to the property's smart features, all of which can be controlled with an iPad or iPhone.

FACING PAGE BOTTOM RIGHT: A circular theme took precedence in the powder room with a bubble shaped glass floor from Italy taking its cue of colors from the artist-designed glass pedestal. The embroidery on the towels, the round sink, the circular rippled-edge mirror, and the sconces all continue the circular theme.

FACING PAGE BOTTOM LEFT: The rosewood door to the powder room implements the starburst design, a unifying motif that is seen throughout the condo. Other doors in the home use oak, primavera, and narra wood to add variety. Directly outside the powder room is a custom, open-faced cabinet created to display a collection of antique Japanese netsukes. The table below is also custom with lacquer sides and granite and glass shelves.

Photographs by Halkin Mason Photography

BIRDSEYE DESIGN

RICHMOND, VT

Working within a historically renovated 1890s gabled barn in Vermont's Huntington Valley, a group of architects, artisans and builders collectively design and craft award-winning custom residential work. Birdseye Design was founded in 1996 and is led by its founding principal architect, Brian J. Mac, AIA. It is the architectural arm of Birdseye Building Company, an employee-owned company featuring general contractors, builders, a cabinet shop, an excavation company and a custom metal shop.

The culture of the firm focuses on the collaboration of designers and makers, working together under one roof to create detailed design solutions for clients. The inherent nature of this tangible exercise facilitates a thoughtfulness of design that is evident throughout the execution of its projects.

As design is the keystone to the firm's success, the unique nature of each home is rooted in a regionalism approach, consistently inspired by context. Birdseye blends and bends the familiar in new directions in response to site and program, and it strives to be inventive in all aspects of design and construction. Through material exploration, construction methods, renewable energy integration and efficient design practices, each home becomes a unique expression of form and function. Clear client communication and strong contractor relationships are of utmost importance in maintaining the high standards of each finished product.

Birdseye works throughout the Northeast and beyond, choosing to work where the art of architecture can be explored with clients who appreciate the process of design, as well as the experience of living in a beautifully inspired space.

"We are rooted in the process of intentional design. We work within the context of creating homes that are specific to client and site. Each line drawn has an embedded meaning that is unique to the project."

—Brian J. Mac

ABOVE: The Cantilever Lake House offers a modern interpretation of the traditional camp aesthetic while maintaining contextual sensitivity. Recessed into the existing hillside, the house avoids an excessively vertical massing while simultaneously creating a walkout lower level adjacent to the lake. Private spaces are situated in the buried portion of the residence, allowing the open, communal spaces to flow directly into the shoreline through the large glass facade. Simple, orthogonal forms, shed roofs, and a minimalist material palette serve to lessen the impact of the house on the waterfront landscape.

FACING PAGE TOP: A 28-foot lift and slide door unit opens to westerly lake views from the living and dining room of the Cantilever House.

FACING PAGE BOTTOM: Parapan cabinet faces and stainless steel details create a harmonious and minimalistic aesthetic to the kitchen design.

PREVIOUS PAGES: Champlain Modern is composed of two angular wings surrounding a central courtyard space and connected by an entry corridor. Large hip roofs with eight-foot eaves define the two wings and create two dramatic 26-foot cantilevered overhangs. The overhangs act to create a series of apertures that frame views along the axis out to the lake. For visitors entering the site, the first overhang frames the courtyard and view of the lake beyond. For occupants in the courtyard, the second overhang frames the cascading path down and the open view to the lake. The material palette is composed of natural materials: western red cedar, Corten cladding, corral board, and board-formed concrete, designed to age gracefully and blend seamlessly into the surroundings.

Photographs by Jim Westphalen

"The successful design of a home is fully realized when there is a common language and seemless layering of the architecture, interiors, and landscape."

—Brian J. Mac

ABOVE LEFT: The Fall Line ski house captures the westerly, panorama view of Sugarbush Ski Resort in the Mad River Valley in the Green Mountains of Vermont. The upper volume of the home is a vernacular gable form cantilevered eight feet in both directions and aligned on axis with the renowned Castlerock Peak, which is known for its steep, narrow, winding, New England-style runs. An office and sitting space above extend out beyond the porch columns.

ABOVE RIGHT: Hand-hewn white oak treads with open risers allow the mountain views to sweep through the stair form. The visual lightness of the structure and heft of the treads create an aesthetic balance within the entry foyer of the house. The stair vertically connects the three living levels of the home together. The reverse living design features bedrooms on the lowest level with the communal areas and the master suite located on the main floor. The office and library are located on the top floor facing the westerly mountain views. The guest suite faces the more private easterly direction.

FACING PAGE TOP: The Fall Line house nestles into the landscape and at the same time projects itself toward the views to the Green Mountains.

FACING PAGE BOTTOM: The large overhangs and cantilevers of the structure reach across the landscape, functioning as protective coverings and as forms blending into the environment.

Photographs by Jim Westphalen

"Visually extending architecture into the landscape, creating organically inspired exteriors, and being consistently harmonious with an idea contribute to the beauty and authenticity of good design."

—Brian J. Mac

ABOVE LEFT: The Quaker Bluff House entry experience is highlighted with a custom Corten steel-edged, bluestone bridge over water. The home's water feature cascades meditatively across the front façade, turns the corner and waterfalls down the side through a series of Corten troughs designed by Wagner Hodgson Landscape Architects. The exterior siding details are compositions of clear vertical grain western red cedar with a custom metal window system.
Photograph by Jim Westphalen

ABOVE RIGHT: The south terrace views look out beyond the generous metal roof overhang, framing a westerly vista to Lake Champlain and the Adirondack Mountains. The black metal custom window system allows for large fixed picture windows, operable awning windows and black panels within the same continuous mullion composition. The interconnectedness of the pattern visually ties the exterior together and creates a harmonious exterior architectural vocabulary.
Photograph by Susan Teare

FACING PAGE TOP: The Quaker Bluff residence transitions elegantly to a two-story walk-out level, using landscape walls, a pergola, a Corten growing wall, and a water feature to integrate the home into the landscape.
Photograph by Susan Teare

FACING PAGE BOTTOM: The Sunset Cliff home's shingle-style aesthetic quietly sits on the bluff of the shore of Lake Champlain.
Photograph by Jim Westphalen

LINDA RUDERMAN INTERIORS

GREENWICH, CT

Look through the portfolio of homes designed by Linda Ruderman Interiors, Inc., and you'll find that the common thread running through the diverse spaces is classical balance. Whether principal Linda Ruderman is commissioned to design modern, contemporary, or period interiors, there is a central symmetry and balance that creates rooms that flow with grace. She particularly loves the challenge of bringing owners' ideas to life and in the end, each home reflects the owners entirely.

Passionate about art and design from a young age—she often rearranged rooms in her family's home as a child—Linda grew up among a family of textile experts. From a very young age, she understood the difference between cotton, silk, linen, and cashmere. She deviated from the work of her father and grandfather, though, when she found that space and layout fascinated her. While in design school, she traveled to various Old World locales: Venice, Morocco, London, the South of France, Istanbul, Milan, and many more, studying the architecture and aesthetics of each destination. When she completed her studies, she worked for an architectural firm before establishing Linda Ruderman Interiors, Inc. That foundation in architecture is apparent in her work, where sculptural pieces, textured draperies, period antiques, and stunning reclaimed materials create an ambiance of the Old World, even in a newly constructed home.

"A home should reflect the people who live within its walls. It should be equally beautiful and functional, and should provide a place for entertainment, respite, and developing relationships."

—Linda Ruderman

ABOVE LEFT & FACING PAGE BOTTOM: A breathtaking view of the water takes center stage in the dining room that boasts a 30-foot ceiling. The custom chandelier is constructed of fiber optics and hand-blown glass. As the eye moves down the chandelier, the hand-blown glass pieces become darker, adding interest to the air space without obstructing the view. The formal living room of the house was kept neutral to allow the beauty of the water to be the focal point. Window treatments, furniture, and finishes are kept in a neutral color palette so you see what's important.
Photographs by Scott Ruderman, Filmmaker & Photographer

ABOVE TOP & BOTTOM RIGHT: The large Moorish-style estate was finished with materials sourced from Morocco. The bedroom suite features laser-cut millwork in a traditional Moorish motif, while the antique tile on the floor was reclaimed from old villas. Peaked arches, crocheted window draperies, and period antiques create a cohesive feel. The adjacent bathroom also features 12-foot ceilings and everything was carefully selected for both rooms.
Photographs by Carmel Brantley, Brantley Photography

FACING PAGE TOP & PREVIOUS PAGES: He wanted a neutral color palette, being from New York. She wanted lots of color, like her home in Mexico. To compromise, splashes of color in the rug and vibrant artwork from the owners' private collection set against a neutral background were combined to create a palette that satisfied both owners. Double doors separate the living room and the dining room beyond when the owners entertain guests. The adjacent foyer was inspired by a beautiful rug pattern, but the pattern on the floor—which is reflected in the ceiling—was achieved by combining Bulgarian limestone and black marble. High-gloss lacquer on the walls gives the interior space a very reflective quality before one transitions to the living area.
Photographs by Tim Williams, Architecture & Interior Design Photography

RONA LANDMAN INTERIOR DESIGN

NEW YORK

Inspired by the 1930s and 1940s, Rona Landman, principal of her eponymous firm, Rona Landman Interior Design, loves creating spaces that surprise and delight. Modifying unique design elements and uncovering hidden architectural gems are just a couple of things for which Rona keeps an eye out. Her style is sophisticated with an air of casual elegance—rooms are often clad in neutral hues to allow for her clients' personal expression and art collections—while only top-notch materials are used to finish the project.

With her one-stop design studio, Rona works with homeowners from a design's inception through completion, as she supervises her entire team of architects, contractors, and expeditors. This allows her clients the luxury of concentrating on the design aesthetics of their beautiful home.

The concept of home is vitally important to Rona—it is the place you return to at the end of the day, and it should be a place for rest, rejuvenation, and entertaining. Home also serves as an owner's personal palette, painting the story of their life through carefully curated pieces, souvenirs from travels, and artwork that touches the soul. When her clients walk into a space that Rona has designed, they feel immediately at home, because it is a true reflection of their hearts and lives.

"Restraint is important. It allows you to showcase favorite pieces and makes a space much more versatile."

—Rona Landman

ABOVE LEFT: The Cast Iron Building was built as a dry goods store called McCreery & Co. in the 1920s. In 1986, the building became a coop with the same 1920s design and style. Now, this New York City loft is a dream come true. The sleek dining room on one side allows for luxurious entertaining. The fixture over the dining table was repurposed from a church, designed by Rona Landman, while the neutral palette provides a gorgeous palette for modern art pieces. Mid-century modern fixtures and furniture were used throughout the home.

ABOVE RIGHT: Originally intended to be a second bedroom, plans had to be altered for the bar space nestled under the second-story bathroom when a gas line was discovered during renovation. The burgundy gives the bar a lounge-like feel and perfectly complements the formal space directly across from it, where a refurbished 1900s Steinway provides music for soirees. The cast iron columns and heavy wood beam in the room were uncovered and highlighted to exaggerate the 15-foot-high ceiling during the renovation, having been covered over when the building was converted to residences in the 1980s.

FACING PAGE: The mezzanine was pushed back to make the living space downstairs feel even more open. The solid brick wall that runs through the entire width of the home needed reinforcement with structural steel to create the largest passageways between the two separate but open living spaces. One side houses a concealed television behind the black-and-white painting. The other houses a fireplace in the more formal space. Glass railing provides an open feeling upstairs, allowing for even more light and space between the main floor and the one above.

PREVIOUS PAGES: Fourteen-foot tall arched windows look out onto the city below and provide ample light to the space. The fireplace, piano, and adjacent bar provide the perfect entertaining space, while a glass-and-steel floating staircase maintains the flow. Guests can move between this room and the sitting room on the other side of the fireplace through two doorways that frame the mid-century modern design.
Photographs by Peter Rymwid

VARENHORST

PHILADELPHIA, PA

Distinctive style, open partnership with clients, and the knowledge necessary for both the renovation of historic homes and the design of new homes make Philadelphia-based Varenhorst a highly-regarded architectural design firm. Led by principal Stephen Varenhorst, the firm has designed and built stunning residences that are both functional and graceful, since 1987. Such designs are Stephen's personal architectural responses to his clients' vision of life. Each design is developed through a series of conversations with the homeowner and provides architectural form to his concerns for space, light, materials, context, and environmental harmony. His work is stylistically flexible, yet devoted to architectural ideas that provide beauty, comfort, and joy to daily life. His experience working with historic homes is significant; his eye for period architecture allows him to bring modern functionality to an older home while preserving the home's original spirit.

Homeowners trust Varenhorst to deliver designs with proper scale, proportions, and a distinct sense of warmth and harmony conducive to their lifestyles. Consistent communication, gentle candor, and dedicated service are hallmarks of the Varenhorst creative process. In addition to traditional architectural design, the team offers planning, feasibility studies, and, through strategic partnerships, lighting design, landscape design and interior design services.

ABOVE & FACING PAGE TOP: The 9,000-square-foot modern residence features an exterior rainscreen design to promote an indoor environment that is virtually allergen-free. An abundance of windows allows natural light to flood the custom home, which features a gourmet kitchen, home theater, stunning master suite, a custom 1,000-gallon saltwater aquarium, and an attached koi pond with a viewing portal from the lower level fitness room.

FACING PAGE BOTTOM: A major renovation corrected the disconnected feeling of the original pinwheel design. Dark and dated interiors were replaced with light and modern elements, such as the wide-plank oak flooring with its contrasting walnut button detail. Alternating floor heights were leveled to allow a natural flow between the kitchen and dining room.

PREVIOUS PAGES: The 1929 stone and Tudor-framed home was purchased by a developer. The homeowner had his team remove the tile roof, salvage and clean the tiles, repair the sagging structure beneath, and meticulously reinstall each tile with a mix of existing and reclaimed tiles. Roof tiles were sourced from across the United States to create a cohesive transition between the old and new. The home now features a four-car garage with an in-law suite above, two-story guest house, theater, gym, family courtyard, outdoor kitchen, and pool.

Photographs by Jeff Totaro

"Design is the expression of a person's lifestyle: how they play, how they work, how they entertain, and how they like to relax. Each element of their lifestyle must be explored to accurately capture their vision."

—Stephen Varenhorst

ABOVE: Respectful of the original 1928 architecture, the new design is conducive to modern living. Rustic wood beams brought in by Amish woodworkers serve as the transition between the sitting area and the kitchen, where friends and family members are welcomed for casual visits.

FACING PAGE TOP: The dining room was opened up to foster better flow for entertaining. Clerestories, glass doors, and expanses of windows provide a delightful connection to the outdoors and give the home a sculptural quality.

FACING PAGE BOTTOM: The 1920s-era home was in need of a renovation. The owner—a furniture designer by trade—desired an open-concept layout with a large, bistro-inspired kitchen. The original warming oven from 1955 was preserved, and a custom hood was added over the stove, behind which an enormous marble slab was installed. The wood-topped island features a raised zinc bar. Beyond the island, a stairway leads to the second floor. Outside, the back terrace steps down to the pool, creating a pleasant outdoor living space.

Photographs by Jeff Totaro

"Architecture is the thoughtful making of space."

—Louis Kahn

Morgante Wilson Architects, page 203

CHAPTER THREE

Nor-Son, page 211

Jackson & McElhaney, page 187

Midwest

CF DESIGN

DULUTH, MN

When an adventurous Minneapolis employer offered a career opportunity to Cheryl Fosdick more than 20 years ago, she took it—and hasn't looked back since. Now nurturing a strong, local residential market, Cheryl has pushed the region's interior taste to new levels as principal designer at CF Design LTD. Strategic and thoughtful, her focus lies in mastering a balance between homeowner and site, pulling geographical factors and personal details to create the perfect space.

Minnesota offers an ideal environment to draw inspiration. The architecture embraces a certain drama found in the state's topography, making open home plans the most appealing and comprehensive. As a distinct intersection of aesthetics, Duluth offers visitors and residents its version of art history, visible in the built form. A transition from shipping port to travel destination over the last two decades has secured Duluth as a thriving possibility for architectural expansion, putting Cheryl's design know-how to work.

"I don't design around any particular style and I don't believe it serves as the essential generator of form. People often become stifled when they think in terms of specific styles."

—Cheryl Fosdick

ABOVE: A window is a frame and a point of departure from the wall. In an open bedroom, the head of the bed supports the canopy of the roof above; the windows then become curtains, defining enclosure. While only the bed is freestanding, the line between architecture and furniture is masterfully blurred.

FACING PAGE: The expression of the opening can define the window as a picture frame for a specific view or a diaphanous fabric of wood and glass, separating inside passages from outside terrain. Light pours through a home's glass, delineating night from day. When used properly, daylight becomes one of the most powerful tools of design. An abstract element becomes almost tangible, as designers have the ability to capture, direct and engineer the sun's rays.

PREVIOUS PAGES: What defines indoor and outdoor? These two environments do not begin and end with walls or partitions. Planes overhead define our limits of a perceived enclosure and the human scale within buildings. People gain comfort from knowing they are under something, surrounded by something—ceilings and walls are structurally believable. Playing off of this notion, ceiling planes that lay low to the ground can present an intimate slice of the surroundings. Essentially limitless on all sides, the space lets residents move easily and see from inside to outside beneath these enduring surfaces.

Photographs by Andrea Rugg

"Don't rush this process. In design, nothing done quickly is ever done well."

—Cheryl Fosdick

ABOVE: Minimalism has many interpretations. One view: it takes very little accommodation to comfortably and specifically inhabit a home. A chair at a table works as a vantage point and an opportunity to set aside time to appreciate the richness of people and place. Sitting in a chair quickly shifts perception. The texture and color of surfaces become more concentrated and pungent when at rest. The design emphasizes the importance of closeness and the contrasting distance of elements under controlled light. In this way, the mass of a fireplace can be interpreted as a mosaic of discreet stones, curiously balanced on the mantel.

FACING PAGE TOP: Creating outward views that include portions of the inhabited residence can camouflage the differences between inside and out. An indoor kitchen and the furniture of its island make up part of the greater outdoor dining space. Guests or homeowners could retire to the pillows of the quiet north court after a meal. A desire for the "place beyond" organizes the site's living spaces into a well-planned assembly.

FACING PAGE BOTTOM: Morning light is often the most poignant. Whether cast through an elegant stairwell or across a bedroom ceiling, morning light works best when the spaces and surfaces are set to receive it. An interior's palette develops through the understanding of daylight's effect: the shadows cast, texture of surfaces and variations of tone changes.
Photographs by Andrea Rugg

"Simple feelings about fundamental things like daylight and the tactile or visual nature of specific materials must be carefully considered, all of which play off of the site and become part of the space."

—Cheryl Fosdick

ABOVE: Inside, simply, the outdoors inspire. Reflecting the dramatically fractured rocks and coulees of the Lake Superior North Shore, the fissured surface of the home's tall wall channels daylight from above, as the redwood stair falls away from the stone shelf of the floor like a river, toward a shaft of light between trees. As if on the water's edge, an embedded reed comprises the rails, along with recycled redwood from a local company. And for an innovative tub design wrapped by a second-floor stairwell clad in redwood, a warm wooden glow is achieved and borrows from the clean beauty of the shower next door. Private and invisible to passersby, the space takes advantage of raw materials and transcends styles to create a carved-out look.

FACING PAGE: When a couple decided to embark on modern design within their home, they knew they were taking a leap of faith. Set on the westernmost point of the Great Lakes, the materials-driven interior selections reflect the nature of the surrounding outdoor elements. The offset third-bond travertine flooring gives a sense of shift and movement to the ground, as a gesture to the water, beach and sand. The design takes advantage of the space's ability to challenge the reality of human scale, juxtaposed with elements intimate as grass and wide as the blue-on-blue horizon lying just beyond the floor-to-ceiling windows.

Photographs by Andrea Rugg

"We are energized by the qualities of the place and remain thoroughly engaged by the landscape. Basalt outcroppings, dramatic inland seas, indistinct horizons of mirrored waters and skies, and leggy white pine forests provide fuel for our imaginations."

—Cheryl Fosdick

ABOVE: The master bedroom is a perfect example of minimizing materials while maximizing the place. Pulling the eye over the distance of the long room, this space treats every attribute as if it were a piece of furniture. Built into the floor and wall, the bed sits with the shower and closet behind it. Not a single square inch is wasted, and supported by extraordinary craftsmanship, design takes center stage.

FACING PAGE TOP: For a rectangular condominium that measures just over 22 by 62 feet, every space is an equal part of a common ground. The whole really is greater than the sum of its parts, as each element—the island, stairways, cabinetry—are related in their furniture-like quality. Under foot and in hand, the same rich redwood that appears on the entry stair and handrail emerges as the wine cask envelops the private second-floor stairway and connects the two levels.

FACING PAGE BOTTOM LEFT: Thoughtfully knitted together, the condominium reveals the intention of each element. Simple things bring the space together: the repetitive vertical grain of the veneered cabinets depends on the horizontal wall pattern going up the stairwell. Contrast and proximity make this all work.

FACING PAGE BOTTOM RIGHT: A small bathroom carves opportunity out of the contrast of stone and glass, filling the space and creating a partition for the shower, both poetic and functional. High-wattage light is bounced to return without shadow to the vanity. Common stone accentuates the delicate and almost transitory nature of the sink and countertop—and of the reflected image in the mirror.

Photographs by Andrea Rugg

ESKUCHE DESIGN

WAYZATA, MN

Established in 2002, Eskuche Design is a boutique residential firm focused on craftsmanship, heirloom quality design and attention to detail in regard to new home construction and extensive renovations. In addition to designing live with the client, founder Peter Eskuche, AIA, also designs from the inside out, paying close attention to the interplay of indoor and outdoor space. With a background in interior design, the architect takes an artful approach to each project as he builds partnerships with clients to design a home that best exudes their personalities.

Throughout the design process the team at Eskuche Design takes the time to get to know a client's story, style, character, organizational habits, artistic desires, as well as how the family operates. This client-focused approach laced with transparency and collaboration renders thoughtful and timeless design, as it enables Peter to create a home that truly radiates the heart of the family.

LEFT: The legacy home took inspiration from a photo of a stairway and a door discovered by the client while vacationing in Monaco. The stairway was recreated on the lakeside of the home with quarried stone from Wisconsin.
Photograph by LandMark Photography

"As we decipher what a client likes about a design image, we want to elevate their inspiration images to a new height by combining elements that really work."

—Peter Eskuche

ABOVE: An elegant Tudor home on Lake Minnetonka effortlessly blends into the site, preserving the natural feel of the property as it offers maximum privacy. The pier was designed for easy access from the family room, while the boathouse takes inspiration from an idyllic Hansel and Gretel cottage.

Photograph by Spacecrafting, Inc.

FACING PAGE: Sited on one of the highest points of the lake, the home features a widow's walk with roof access that provides stunning views of the lake's 200-mile shoreline. Four types of stone, all quarried from nearby Wisconsin, make up the complexion of the exterior. Triple-glazed windows with a high UV filter help contain the interior's warmth, as they maximize enjoyment of the water.

Photograph by LandMark Photography

"I spent my boyhood dreaming up tree houses, quirky spaces, and impossible shelter designs. I think all those random dreams helped me build the creative resources to interpret my clients' dreams."

—Peter Eskuche

ABOVE: A pool house constructed of rough cedar on Lake Minnetonka incorporates the best of indoor and outdoor living, as it features a protected outside kitchen and fire pit. A roll-down screen and a roll-down clear vinyl wall give the clients options as to how to enjoy the space throughout the seasons.

Photograph by Scott Amundson Photography

FACING PAGE TOP: Elegant design gives the East Coast-inspired home seaside sophistication. Inspired by calm coastal design, the Lake Minnetonka home exudes the feel of summer year-round, as it features modern home amenities and detailing. Articulated surfaces are purposely designed into the home with a surprising dichotomy of styles, perfect for an active family.

Photograph by Scott Amundson Photography

FACING PAGE BOTTOM: Indoor-outdoor living was imperative in the design, as the home faces east on the lake—think glorious sunrises. An infinity-edge pool further frames the view, promoting more outdoor activity and relaxation.

Photograph by Scott Amundson Photography

FRANCE LAVIN DESIGN

MILWAUKEE, WI

Luxury and comfort go hand-in-hand, especially when you're talking about the designs of France Lavin, principal of France Lavin Design, Inc. Homes across the United States have been graced by France's keen eye for detail with a touch of glamour, but it was a home that she just happened upon in Naples, Florida, that started her on her current path. When her new home caught the eye of one of Naples' premier magazines—after it had been completely renovated—word quickly spread and France found herself in demand. It's not just her design acumen that draws clients to her, however, but also her creative and approachable manner.

France is as patient as she is fun-loving, and enjoys getting to know homeowners over a cup of coffee or glass of wine before starting a project. Once underway, she expertly guides clients through the design process in a way that's unequivocally fun and inspired. There are always special details in France's designs, whether it's a piece of furniture designed and built for the space, or a surprising mix of metals and textures, no matter the budget. She makes the most of a room, reusing elements when necessary, and always bringing in something unexpected. You'll often find mirrors in her designs, as they add life to a room. Their presence there is a bit metaphorical for homeowners too; she designs rooms that perfectly reflect her clients' personalities and lifestyles in a timeless way.

LEFT: A one-of-a-kind dining table takes center stage in the dining area of an unaffected but elegant condo. The undulating edge of the glass tabletop mimics live edge tables constructed of split wood logs, while the stacked reclaimed wood base adds a contemporary twist to the design. Classic barn doors draw the eye to the angled doorway; hardwood floors and oversized trim ground the space.
Photograph by John Kimple

ABOVE: The Cherry Creek penthouse was the owner's opportunity to completely recreate her vision for what home should look like, so we took an "architecture to accessories" approach to create an entirely new feel by designing everything from the room's structure to the smallest decorative elements. A mix of metals and finishes delights in the space: nearly-black metal around the fireplace, the hammered antique gold coffee table, and the cascading crystal and chrome chandelier over the dining table. Raspberry-red swivel chairs provide flexible seating next to the luxurious Italian leather sectional. The high black lacquer bar—designed specifically for the room—holds all of the owner's crystal and fine china. Mahogany medallion-shaped dining chairs feature an off-center black stripe on the back, adding another glamourous touch.
Photograph by Victor Sanchez

FACING PAGE TOP LEFT: The existing vanity in a Lakewood master bath was removed while new floors were installed. The vanity was then mounted on the wall about six inches higher than before, creating the illusion that it's floating. Under cabinet lighting adds a little something extra, while the huge mirror above the vanity visually expands the space. Four wall sconces were mounted directly onto the mirror, and a mirrored medicine cabinet hangs over each sink.
Photograph by Linda Hanselman

FACING PAGE TOP RIGHT: The contemporary kitchen in a Milwaukee waterfront condo is the perfect example of mixing masculine and feminine elements. The bubbly "egg sculpture" beside the window is eye-catching without being intimidating. Scandinavian bar stools along the bar mold around your body when you sit, and above the bar, lights mounted in solid chunks of crystal reflect light throughout the kitchen. They're like the room's jewelry and very feminine. In contrast, the black-and-white painting in the background features a very masculine motorcyclist, balancing out the more feminine aspects of the design.
Photograph by John Kimple

FACING PAGE BOTTOM: Original floral chalk art in oversized matting and frames hang on either side of the black wrought iron bed to draw attention to the architecture and symmetry of the piece in this master bedroom. A mixture of grays and metallic silver bedding gives the black bed a sexy feel, and a silvery chaise lounge adds another soft surface for relaxing. The feminine aspects of the room, like the frilly pillow that sits on the chaise, create a striking contrast with weightier pieces—the black lamp shades, black wrought iron—on the opposite side of the room. The monochromatic space is soothing and almost spa-like.
Photograph by John Kimple

JACKSON & MCELHANEY

AUSTIN, TX

Each client and each site present a new challenge in design, but that is what the team at Austin-based Jackson & McElhaney love about what they do. Taking into account everything from the angle of the sun to the direction of the natural breezes a site offers, the firm designs homes that reflect the unique characteristics of location as well as the lifestyle of the homeowners. Whether they're looking for a home that feels like a compound that's been in the family for decades or an urban retreat that blends harmoniously with nature, clients trust Jackson & McElhaney to bring their visions to life.

Founded in 1975 as Robert Jackson Architects, Jackson & McElhaney has created an extensive portfolio of residential and commercial projects primarily in Central Texas. Each home is built with an eye toward preserving the environment and using energy in the most passive way possible. Recognized for its energy-efficient construction methods, Jackson & McElhaney was green before it became a buzzword. The firm boasts several five-star Austin Energy Green Building homes and follows current best practices in efficient building, and earned the prestigious *Top 10 Green Building Award* in 2006. The firm's associations with the Sustainable Building Coalition and LEED Green Building speak volumes for the importance the team places on the environment.

It is the holistic care with which the architects at Jackson & McElhaney approach a project that brings clients back to them time and again. The firm's goal is to provide owners with a home that is as economically wise as it is beautiful. Simple alignment and straightforward features like custom overhangs, strategic window placement, and the industrious use of screened porches create homes that are environmentally responsible and as unique as the people who reside within them.

"Sunlight can be your best friend or your biggest enemy. It's all in how you design a structure around that light."

—Michael McElhaney

ABOVE: The owners named their home Shungyo-An, which means "Spring Dawn" in Japanese. The home is aligned perfectly with the spring equinox. The design of Shungyo-An allows beautiful morning sunlight to flood the interiors in the spring, yet shields the home from the heat of the summer. A catwalk on the second floor provides a thoroughfare from one end of the home to another while maintaining views of the outdoors.
Photograph courtesy of Greg Hursley

FACING PAGE TOP LEFT: The Hyde Park home near downtown Austin, Texas is in a very urban neighborhood, but that doesn't prevent the owners from moving their bed out onto the second-story deck to enjoy nature and sleep out under the stars.
Photograph courtesy of Ryann Ford

FACING PAGE TOP RIGHT: The Lake Travis home is situated on a hill with many houses below it. To eliminate the view of the rooflines, the pool extends out from the house and appears to end right where the lake begins.
Photograph courtesy of Robert Jackson

FACING PAGE BOTTOM RIGHT: Windows run along the side of the living room and dining room of a home that sits along the Blanco River. Concrete floors and a concrete fireplace surround contrast with the natural wood slat ceiling that helps absorb some of the sounds in the home.
Photograph courtesy of Robert Jackson

FACING PAGE BOTTOM LEFT: To create a compound-like feel to the home, traditional farmhouse elements and a curved screened porch add character to the courtyard-like backyard where family gathers to splash in the pool. There's a rambling feel to the home, as if it were added onto over the years, but in reality, it's new construction.
Photograph courtesy of Greg Hursley

PREVIOUS PAGES: Stone barns are rare in Central Texas, so adding onto a limestone barn built in 1941 was certainly an exciting project. The barn was preserved and the residence was expanded to include home offices for the couple, separated by a screened porch. Dormer windows were added to the barn's upstairs where the living room and kitchen are located. The original steel roof now serves as the ceiling upstairs. The home is now protected from the elements with added insulation and a new steel roof on the exterior. At the center of the home is a screened porch that works like an old fashioned dog trot. Even during the height of summer, the breeze moving through the space cuts energy costs by keeping it cool.
Photograph courtesy of Stephen Knetig with 360 Premier Tours

LAUREN COBURN

CHICAGO, IL

Lauren Coburn has a strong architectural and design background, which shines through in each of her projects. She founded her firm after completing her interior architecture studies at the School of the Art Institute of Chicago and following extensive work with renowned firms Tigerman McCurry Architects and Soucie Horner Ltd. Through her education and experiences, Lauren grew to appreciate the importance of the working relationship among the architect, designer, and homeowner and learned how to foster the cohesive, productive, and creative team that every successful project needs. Today, Lauren and her firm create stunning, highly personalized, residences as well as a line of custom furniture pieces.

A hallmark of Lauren's designs is that her interiors do not have one particular style or look. Indeed, each home that Lauren works on achieves a strong sense of beauty by customizing the space and taking the homeowner's wants and needs into account. For example, for a six-foot, nine-inch homeowner, Lauren and her team factored his height into every detail, from high ceilings and countertops to bespoke furniture. Similarly, when another homeowner wanted to show off his modern art, Lauren and her team ensured that his collection was represented throughout the home and served as the focal point in several integrated installations. Lauren and her team never lose sight of the fact that in the end, it's all about the homeowner's comfort and tastes, which Lauren translates and implements into beautiful living spaces with her extraordinary design skills and eye for detail.

"Every element is created with the homeowner in mind. The space must make sense for a particular lifestyle."
—Lauren Coburn

TOP, CENTER, & BOTTOM: Set in a scenic Illinois suburb, a traditional estate that originally had a dark, heavy interior was completely transformed. Incorporating the owner's desire for a coastal feel gave the home an airy, light concept. The soft palette of whites and blues helped achieve a beach-inspired feel with a strong calming effect. A collection of vibrant modern art and customized, over-scaled furniture pieces—primarily created by Lauren—highlights the home's elegance. While the striking, mainly modern art adds contrast to the home's traditional elements, the loosely French-inspired custom furniture brought in the homeowner's personal vision. And since three young children and two dogs live in the home, Lauren used practical and beautiful stain-resistant fabrics throughout the space.

FACING PAGE: Lauren designed the Gold Coast home to let natural light pour in and show off its striking architectural details and design elements. Crisp and white, the dining space uses mirrors to reflect the light from the nearby window, while open shelves on the kitchen wall let light flow uninterruptedly from the corner window.

PREVIOUS PAGES: When a creative director for a high-profile Chicago company hired Lauren to renovate his vintage duplex on Chicago's Gold Coast, Lauren wanted to match his high expectations of drama and beauty. The firm succeeded masterfully, with an effective, eye-catching use of black and white contrast. The 1925 Gothic Revival building had some beautiful elements—including floor-to-ceiling windows, original glass, the staircase, and interior doors—which needed substantial restoration to preserve the character of the space. The black-and-white mixed media artwork is by Barbara Coburn.

Photographs by Tony Soluri Photography © 2015 Lauren Coburn, LLC

Art Nouveau
Art Nouveau

ABOVE & FACING PAGE TOP: When most people think of media rooms, large screens and theater seating come to mind, but when Lauren was selected to design the media room for the Merchandise Mart Dream Home, she took a different approach. With the modern family in mind—and the understanding that some people don't have the space for an extra media room—Lauren designed a dual-purpose formal living room/media room. Starting with an antique credenza under the large flat screen, Lauren designed two matching rosewood units that each house smaller televisions that can be watched simultaneously through the use of headphones. Electrical sliding panels cover the smaller televisions when not in use, but are attached to sensors, so they raise when someone enters the room. Luminous wood veneer in a scroll pattern covers the wall behind the television and the sofa sitting opposite. The artwork was created by Lauren's mother, Michigan artist Barbara Coburn.
Photographs courtesy of Lauren Coburn and the Merchandise Mart

FACING PAGE BOTTOM: Vintage and new pieces complement one another in the eclectic living room. Beautiful shades of gold, cocoa, and cream mingle with black vintage Asian stools and the African artifact on the mantle. The silver hammered metal and white glass Bradley étagères features the owner's milk glass collection complemented by eye-catching accessories. The bronze and glass coffee table, also by Bradley, adds yet another sculptural focal point to the room. A soft rug by Oscar Isberian Rugs grounds the space, and the lines of the sofa, from Jayson Home are mirrored in the graceful chair in front of the arched window. Barbara Coburn original pieces flank the fireplace, adding even more light to the space.
Photograph by Tony Soluri Photography © Lauren Coburn, LLC

MORGANTE-WILSON ARCHITECTS

EVANSTON, IL

With an emphasis on the celebration of living, Morgante-Wilson Architects focuses on developing structures that create memories for families. To these architects, it's not just a house. It's a place to cook dinner, play games, watch movies and simply enjoy each other's company. Founders Elissa Morgante and Fred Wilson incorporate this mantra into each project, resulting in a fun and fulfilling experience for all involved.

Elissa and Fred believe that being happy in your home allows for happiness in other areas of life. One way they achieve this is by translating architecture and its various languages for clients. This exercise allows the seasoned team at Morgante-Wilson Architects to interpret a client's vision, needs and wants into a structure that facilitates their lifestyle, as it integrates core design principles. By developing a strong dialog from the initial meeting, the client feels a sense of ownership in the process that only strengthens the relationship they have for their home.

This approach to design has fostered long-lasting friendships across the country, in addition to multiple projects for families ranging from vacation homes to empty nester dwellings. Regardless of the type of residential structure, Morgante-Wilson Architects stays true to its philosophy and the positive experience it brings to life.

"Our designs are a celebration of living. We want to help families create memories for generations to come. Designing a structure that works with a family's lifestyle is the best way to achieve that."

—Fred Wilson

ABOVE & PREVIOUS PAGES: Sited on Wisconsin's Lake Green, the legacy home celebrates its natural setting by bringing nature into the space at every opportunity. Upon entering the home, water greets you, as the lakeside of the home features expansive windows. A four-season porch, complete with heated floors and storm panels, allows nature to entertain with sunsets, as well as snowstorms. The street façade of the Green Lake home is in keeping with the context of the neighborhood. Garages flank the home's porte-cochere, while a grass courtyard offers additional parking for guests. Pac-Clad roofing punctuates the richness of the design.

FACING PAGE TOP: Indigenous stone cut in various sizes adds texture and interest. A large slab of marble serves as an artistic focal point, while white oak floors round out the freshness of the space.

FACING PAGE BOTTOM: A bridge spans across the home, exuding the appearance of a virtual ceiling. The aesthetic is a result of the home's engineering, as steel enforcements were a must in order to combat the strong winds coming off of the lake. Instead of burying them in the wall, the team offered a new translation of the lake lodge language, blurring the line between contemporary and vernacular.

Photographs by Werner Straube Photography

"We focus on helping the homeowner understand what they want in a home. It's important to listen and help them understand what they're looking for, what the spaces will feel like and how they can be used in a variety of ways."
—Elissa Morgante

TOP: The vacation home in Avon, Colorado, is an edgy and contemporary design solution that adheres to the neighborhood's height restraints and various restrictions. This is the fourth project the firm has done for the family, earning Elissa and Fred the title of "family architect."

BOTTOM: A floating staircase coupled with a dry-set masonry wall adds a sculptural element to the home.

FACING PAGE TOP: Views of the ski runs at Beaver Creek and Vail, as well as the mountains and sky, were the driving forces of the design. The family room is open to the kitchen and dining area, creating a large space for the family to congregate and experience the view together.

FACING PAGE BOTTOM: The view can be enjoyed from the stand-alone tub in the master bath, as the space features automated blinds. Placing the vanity across from the window enlarges the space and further enhances the experience of being in the Rocky Mountains.

Photographs by Gideon Photography

"The seamless development of interior design adds a rich layer to the architecture."

—Elissa Morgante

RIGHT: A curved stairwell climbs two stories with a glass handrail topped with wood. It sits in the entry of the townhome, along with a stunning stonewall accented with live edge wood and enlivened with light boxes embedded into the wall. To the left of the space is a wine room.

FACING PAGE TOP: A Chicago townhome offers a contemporary, yet warm, environment for empty nesters. Though construction had begun on what was originally a less-than desirable floor plan, the couple, a repeat client of Morgante-Wilson Architects, purchased the raw space and did a complete overhaul. Located on the second floor, the main living space now works beautifully for city living.

FACING PAGE BOTTOM: The townhome's kitchen is all about materiality. Two marble slabs serve as backsplashes for the space that is further enhanced with walnut floors and cerused white oak detailing. Crossed metal bars on the island caps accent the stainless steel detailing of the appliances and fixtures.

Photographs by Werner Straube Photography

NOR-SON

WAYZATA, MN

Founded in 1978, Nor-Son successfully integrates architecture and construction to provide the highest level of craftsmanship and personal attention possible during the custom homebuilding process. Leveraging both in-house and outside architects, Nor-Son's award-winning architecture and construction team delivers environments of distinctive character and incomparable quality.

Exemplary projects involve a complex blend of people, relationships, ideas, creativity, decisions and solutions. People who design need to understand and complement those who build. Nor-Son's integrated approach promotes open communication and collaboration with team members to accurately blend form, function, aesthetics and costs towards a successful project completion. From conceptualization to virtual renderings to reality, Nor-Son's architects work in concert with construction experts, giving design creativity a firm grounding in construction reality. This philosophy renders beautifully comfortable homes that fully illustrate the client's vision and Nor-Son's expertise.

ABOVE & PREVIOUS PAGES: The Forever Estate on Lake Minnetonka was designed for making memories for a lifetime. By combining design elements from French provincial and countryside cottage architecture, Nor-Son's team created a distinctive home that will stand the test of time. While limestone is a typical exterior material, Nor-Son repurposed its application, as each stone has a unique shape, molded into custom and intricate design details. The pool area perfectly frames a breathtaking view of Lake Minnetonka, as it also serves as an outdoor focal point. A 30-foot span from the living room further frames the view, offering access to the pool as it features a phantom screen that offers protection from insects and high winds.

RIGHT: A coffered ceiling with a subtle arch gives the music room a warm, yet luxurious feel. A transitional chandelier punctuates the space's elegant gray hues, as does the glass wall of windows facing the lake.

FACING PAGE: The infinity symbol was incorporated into the home's design to further illustrate the "forever home" idea. The symbol subtly appears in the custom iron stair rail and can also be found throughout the home in the master bath tile and pool area. *Photographs by Spacecrafting Inc.*

"Many of our clients have built innovative, successful businesses so they appreciate innovation in a design and construction process. We focus on a high-touch experience combined with a high-tech delivery and that's what results in a high performance structure."

—Scott Kuehl

ABOVE: The modern craft home is built on the banks of a lake in northern Minnesota. Far from rustic, the interior successfully incorporates an abundance of natural light, clean lines and earth tones that provoke a sense of tranquility.

FACING PAGE TOP: The home incorporates natural elements such as Douglas fir timber columns, maple flooring, rain glass doors, and stone tile.

FACING PAGE BOTTOM: Constructed in a beautifully crafted farmhouse style, the home boasts clean, modern architecture with natural elements to create a contemporary yet warm and welcoming environment—perfectly suited for lake living.

Photographs by Scott Amundson

OPTIMA

CHICAGO, IL

Three decades ago, David Hovey established Optima with a revolutionary approach to creating architecture and the belief that quality pays for itself. He is involved in every phase of the development process and utilizes the best people, techniques, and materials to create epic results. With more than 20 high-end multifamily residences to his credit, David employs a stellar team of architects, engineers, construction managers, real estate brokers, property managers, accountants, and financial analysts. These professionals work together to efficiently and effectively bring his visions to life.

Perhaps inspired by his native New Zealand, which is comprised of two small islands that possess as much ecological diversity as the entire United States, David designs his projects to celebrate the beauty of nature. His architecture is decidedly site-specific, designed to maximize the locale's views, climate, and culture. It speaks to the beauty of form and the practicality of function, all in a forward-minded way. The buildings David and his team create are designed for the here and now to enhance the day-to-day rhythms of life.

"Beauty is derived from simplicity. In order for a building to be truly great and architecturally significant it must be beautiful, function well, and be structurally sound. All are equally important."

—David Hovey

RIGHT: With 42 stories of shimmering glass, Optima Chicago Center proves itself a sophisticated complement to the city's famed skyline. Featuring striking contemporary style inside and out, the multifamily building is designed to foster a sense of community, connecting residents with one another and to the city as a whole.

FACING PAGE TOP: The sky garden terrace frees residents to connect with the city while relaxing amid thoughtful landscaping. In addition to the dramatic infinity-edge pool and lounge area, the terrace features an array of seating areas for intimate conversations as well as get-togethers for larger groups.

FACING PAGE BOTTOM & PREVIOUS PAGES: Floor-to-ceiling glass is a defining characteristic of Optima Chicago Center. The building's prime downtown location deserves to be celebrated with panoramic views from every residence and common area.

Photographs courtesy of Optima

"Design is a constant challenge to balance comfort with luxe, the practical with the desirable."

—Donna Karan

Lori Carroll & Associates, page 287

CHAPTER FOUR

Maria Ogrydziak Architecture, page 297

Gelotte Hommas Architecture, page 269

West

ALLEN-GUERRA ARCHITECTURE

BRECKENRIDGE, CO

Thoughtful, creative, detail oriented, and well-traveled, Suzanne Allen Sabo, founder of Allen-Guerra Architecture, builds homes that are truly unique. Through the integration of surprising styles and interesting materials, Suzanne and her team of architects, engineers, and artists create livable works of art by listening to their clients' wishes and bringing them into reality. With offices in both Breckenridge, Colorado, and Houston, Texas, Allen-Guerra Architecture has designed houses and planned ranches across the country and as far away as New Zealand and Egypt.

Joined by a team with diverse talents and backgrounds—lead designer and project manager Timothy Sabo is an artist and musician; lead architect Yves Mariethoz, AIA, NCARB hails from Switzerland—Suzanne carefully considers both the site and homeowners' lifestyles when building a residence. The result is a home that's warm, elegant, and simply feels good. Homeowners return to Allen-Guerra time and again, not only for exceptional service, but also for the friendships that Suzanne and the team build while building their homes.

"A linear home doesn't have to be boring. When blended seamlessly into the environment, it becomes a work of art."

—Suzanne Allen Sabo

RIGHT: Floor-to-ceiling glass makes up the back façade of the home. When visitors enter via the front door, they can look through the entire structure, past the grand piano, and out the back windows to the incredible view of the slopes.

PREVIOUS PAGES: Unusual and complex materials combined to make the home truly one of a kind. Part French Medieval, part Palm Springs modern, and part mountain rustic, the home features walnut doors and steel accents throughout. The home was designed in a very linear fashion in order to capitalize on the incredible Breckenridge area views. A combination of Douglas fir timbers and steel was used to create the frame, which supports a great deal of the home's structural load. Lacquered and waxed finishes preserve the natural state of the steel, giving it a more authentic look than a typical steel powder finish.

Photographs by Marie Dominique Verdier

"Bringing the outdoors in is more than just flooding the space with natural light. It's the mingling of stone, wood, steel, and the human elements that make it a truly special integration."

—Suzanne Allen Sabo

ABOVE LEFT & ABOVE RIGHT: Barn doors at the hall between the catering kitchen, pantry, and bar allow the owners to close off parts of the home when entertaining. Nine-foot entry doors to the primary suite were custom designed by the firm and lead into the owners' retreat, flooded with natural light. Reclaimed European oak flooring with a natural, matte finish runs throughout the home.

FACING PAGE TOP: Custom walnut and zinc cabinets feature a one-of-a-kind cabinet design that includes a waney edge to the walnut boards, which was juxtaposed with the sleek zinc inlay. A steel cantilevered bar countertop extends into the floor system to provide more structural support, while Colorado grey granite with a drystack application adds sculptural interest.

FACING PAGE BOTTOM: The piano became a natural centerpiece of the home, positioned between the great room and the dining room. It is also centered on the front door, so it's the first thing visitors see when they walk into the home.

Photographs by Marie Dominique Verdier

"The best modern homes have a flow that's easy, warm, and comfortable."
—Suzanne Allen Sabo

LEFT: All granite walls and reclaimed European oak combine to make one feel enveloped by nature when walking down the hallway.

ABOVE: The exterior of the home is clad in Colorado fir and pine that were put through a special aging process to give them more character. Granite grounds the façade.

FACING PAGE BOTTOM: The open floorplan allows for easy movement throughout the common areas, which extend for more than 70 feet.
Photographs by Marie Dominique Verdier

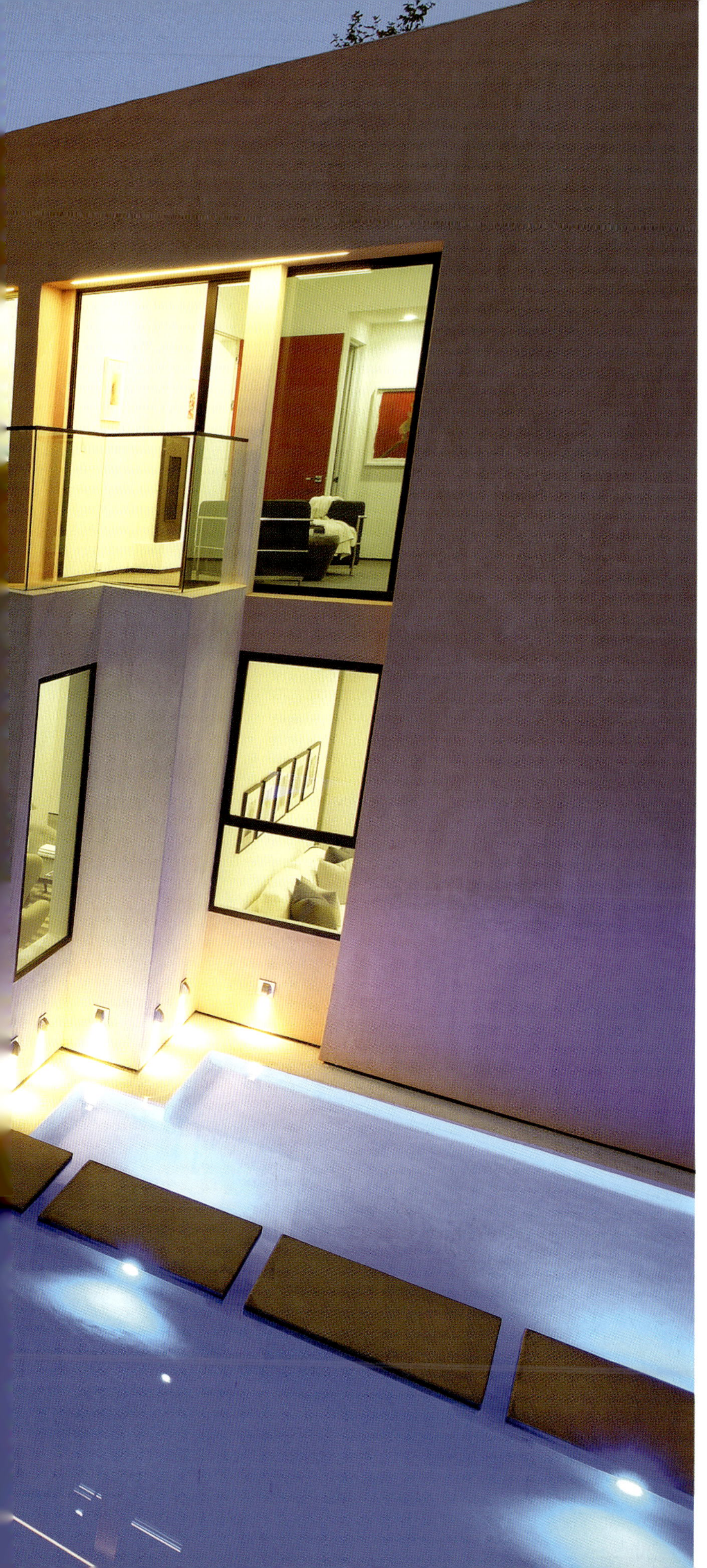

AMIT APEL DESIGN

WOODLAND HILLS, CA

Raised in Africa, Israel, and Europe, Amit Apel enjoys learning and experiencing various cultures. This lust for adventure led him to Southern California in 1999 where the fifth-generation exterior and interior designer purchased a modest Honda Magnum motorcycle to travel across the USA for three months. After his adventurous, cross-country tour and with little means, he opened a humble, 100-square-foot art studio within a locksmith shop on the beaches of Malibu. He instantly became a local, buzz-worthy artist.

A year later, he opened Amit Apel Design and now partners with architect Michael MacLaren. Together their team works with professionals throughout the world to create award-winning commercial, residential and interior designs in Europe, Asia, South America, and the United States. Regardless of where the project is located, the approach begins by translating the client's vision. Throughout the design process the team utilizes everything from the site to indigenous materials to create spaces that surprise and nourish the soul.

LEFT: The Beverly Hills residence was not built on a desirable site. Negative aspects of the property were turned into positives through the design of a structure that looks into itself. The pool hugs the house while various elevations of balconies and terraces add interest in addition to a host of angles in unexpected places.
Photograph courtesy of Amit Apel Design

"Utilizing the space is key in creating a calm and natural environment."
–Amit Apel

TOP: Constructed by Gilad Avidor, the home incorporated lots of angles to create the illusion of more depth and size. Instead of disconnecting the retaining wall from the site, it becomes an integral part of the design that is embraced by the interior. The kitchen's ceiling soars approximately 20 feet, allowing the space to be viewed by the second floor mezzanine.

MIDDLE: A glass-enclosed wine cellar adds interest to the space, while outdoor dining blends into the environment seamlessly. Rectangles pervade the space, exuding a clean and fresh environment.

BOTTOM: The master bath features a custom concrete tub, as well as more angles to connect it to the architectural language of the home. Refurbished wood adds texture as it enhances the rich elegance of the room.

FACING PAGE TOP: A West Hollywood home built on a square lot incorporates shadows and angles to make a statement. Working with developer Anchor Homes and the construction company Anchor Project Services, and its owner Matt Ediger, the architect placed the front door in the middle of the site and incorporated the yard into the design's interior. The garage sits in the front of the house creating a new angle line that inspires intrigue.

FACING PAGE BOTTOM: Angling the tiles in the stairwell gives the space energy and excitement. Pure steel stairs serve as a sculptural element, while the pool and patio are treated as integral parts of the home's interior. Each visit offers a new architectural surprise.

Photographs courtesy of Amit Apel Design

DEAN LARKIN DESIGN

WEST HOLLYWOOD, CA

Described as the quintessential Los Angeles architect, Dean Larkin, AIA, grew up appreciating the natural beauty of his southern California surroundings. It is this enduring admiration that continues to influence every project he designs at his eponymous firm. Established in 1999, Dean Larkin Design maximizes the intrinsic potential of a setting while meeting each client's specific lifestyle, business, or institutional needs.

With no room for predictable plans, Dean transcends the ordinary in his portfolio of high-end residential, commercial, and luxury destination projects that are an expressive reflection of both the people who inhabit them and the natural landscape. An innovative balance between shadow and light, movement and stillness, and form and function all evoke the distinctive climate, attitude, and personality of each project while also bridging the interior with the exterior to compellingly celebrate the splendor of the great outdoors.

LEFT: The dramatic knife-edge pool, illuminated with color-changing LED lights, is undoubtedly one of the most striking, wow factors, as it hugs every curve of the home. It is virtually a kinetic work of art connecting earth and sky and the interior with the exterior. One can quite literally step from the living area through a sliding wall of glass and into the water.
Photograph courtesy of Dean Larkin Design

"Great architecture does more than just work—it transcends itself, its occupants, and its environment."

—Dean Larkin

ABOVE: Perched in the exclusive Bird Streets neighborhood of the Hollywood Hills, the 6,000-square-foot Bluejay residence was completely re-imagined to maximize the site's sweeping Los Angeles views while reflecting the homeowner's trendsetting lifestyle. The open-plan great room includes a living area and a long wraparound bar that is made for communal seating and entertaining. Behind the bar, a vertical stainless steel wine refrigerator extends all the way to the ceiling, thus providing a seamless way to solve for the lack of a wine room in the home. The LED lighting underneath the countertops echoes the mood of the pool yet again uniting the indoor and outdoor spaces.

FACING PAGE TOP: The master suite was relocated to the main level to integrate more fully into the entertainment complex of the home, likewise taking full advantage of the pool. A covered seating lounge with a custom-designed outdoor sofa bed extends the sleeping area outside, where the continuation of the bedroom's stained walnut ceilings and floors also blurs the lines between the inside and outside.

FACING PAGE BOTTOM: While the property sits directly on the street, a walled-in entry sequence creates a sense of drama and privacy while setting the tone for the rest of the space. The limestone pathway, lit from underneath, appears to be floating as it entrancingly guides the way to the front door.

Photographs courtesy of Dean Larkin Design

"A magical convergence of design occurs when the exterior and the interior engage each other in a most dynamic way."

—Dean Larkin

ABOVE: Also located in the Bird Streets, the Swallow residence practically takes flight with its soaring roof lines and enlightening glass walls. Designed for a client in the fashion industry who wanted the home to convey a strong sense of style and personality, the 8,000-square-foot contemporary stunner was built in an L-shape around the oasis of the front yard and its front-facing views. The pool seamlessly connects with the living room, directly engaging with the area before cascading down towards the street level.

FACING PAGE TOP: Embracing a midcentury modern ease while also transcending it, the home oozes with a timeless sense of old and new. The stone walls bring the outside in while acting as monumental relics as they interact with the sleekly streamlined undercurrent of the light-filled rooms.

FACING PAGE BOTTOM: At first glance, this light-filled haven perhaps would never be assumed to be the master bathroom. Truly a sanctuary, the space is nothing short of a Zen experience—from the disappearing glass walls, to the sunken tub that looks out onto the water feature and gardens, and the artfully floating vanity. The repetition of the stone walls reinforces a grounded sense of timelessness that is at once fresh and modern yet evocative of a storied European aesthetic.

Photographs courtesy of Dean Larkin Design

ABOVE: To bring the Macapa residence into the 21st century and capitalize on its jaw-dropping 270-degree views, a complete overhaul was in order. Nicknamed "the flying wing" by the original architect Harry Gesner, the dated structure was liberated from its heavy, windowless design, rising like a phoenix from the ashes to have one of the more iconic silhouettes in the Hollywood Hills. Both the master suite on the ground floor and the second-floor living area and sizable entertaining deck showcase a whole new level of transparency, enticingly encompassing the panoramic vista that extends from the famous Hollywood sign to downtown Los Angeles to the ocean beyond. Even the color palette of the property celebrates its natural surroundings; the white cedar and earthy tone-on-tone hues reflect the native bedrock and dirt upon which the home is built.

FACING PAGE TOP: The transformation began with the very entrance to the 4,000-square-foot home, where a water feature on the stone wall and linear rows of grass in the pavement create something of a peaceful, Zen-like refuge. Because the home features a flipped floor plan, with the main living and entertaining spaces on the second floor, a front staircase was installed with LED risers to usher the way upstairs.

FACING PAGE BOTTOM: The master bathroom boasts one of the most incredible views around, where the freestanding tub is surrounded by LaCantina bi-fold doors that nearly disappear, blurring the line between inside and outside. Yet they are also configured to become opaque for privacy, as desired. The house previously had no yard, so a new green space was created through a series of retaining walls.

Photographs courtesy of Dean Larkin Design

DEBRA MAY HIMES INTERIOR DESIGN

PHOENIX, AZ

An award-winning interior designer, Debra May Himes has served the residential and commercial design fields since 1975 while also creating high-end, original custom furniture. Recently named one of Arizona's top interior designers, her diverse range of projects includes hospitals, corporate buildings, law firms, and banks along with model homes and custom homes. While her design services encompass everything from space planning to furniture and finish selection along with design development drawings and project management, what she is most passionate about is delivering unique ideas and problem-solving solutions that are truly impactful and personalized for her clients.

Signature to her aesthetic is the creation of striking entrances and additional interior architectural details that provide for dramatic focal points while making a statement and setting the tone for the rest of the space. Materials and furnishings are woven together in contrasting yet complementary ways to add visual interest and intrigue. It all serves to develop a significant wow factor—one that has led her work to be described as elegant, livable, and emotionally compelling.

Debra's drive for fresh and exceptional furniture inspired her own furniture line, Jonathan David—named after her two sons—which is designed and customized specifically for her clients and other designers across the country.

Debra's accreditations and affilliations include ASID, IIDA, LEED AP, and NCIDQ certified.

"The beauty of design is in making a room unique, special, and personally intuitive."

—Debra May Himes

TOP: The mountain retreat's master bedroom was designed to reflect the ambience of a luxury resort. The headboard wall of the bed is composed of panels of wood upholstered in leather and installed in a layered manner for added dimensionality. The fireplace is detailed in copper cladding on a brick pattern with clavos accents. The copper motif is likewise repeated in the bowed nightstands and the lamps, which are constructed from copper vases—both of which Debra designed for the space.

BOTTOM: Like the master bedroom, the master bath is nothing short of resort-quality with a luxurious spa-like mood. The slate tiles feature an inset of river rock for an organic finish while the pattern above the tub represents the fluidity of a wave.

FACING PAGE: The statement-making black river rock fireplace commands attention as the focal point of the great room. It is built out from the flat wall for added dimension and topped with iron and lit onyx, which becomes something of an art piece. The design immediately directs the eye upwards to the ceiling that was once a standard rectangle structure but was intriguingly transformed through beams with metal mesh detail.

PREVIOUS PAGES: This family room in North Scottsdale balances a focal point wall that features a honed golden green slate fireplace and entertainment area with the adjacent striking view to the scenery outside. The Jonathan David furniture pieces combine sophisticatedly bold lines with buttery rich coziness and were designed specifically for this space. Light and air work around and through the structure of the tables, which unite walnut, glass, and copper to impactful effect. The fireplace echoes the copper theme in its linear bands, imbuing the space with additional cohesiveness. All elements were designed in harmony to produce a sense of tranquil beauty melded with a comfortable, homey feel.

Photographs courtesy of Debra May Himes Interior Design & Associates

"A touch of the dramatic is a great way to create an interesting, impactful space."

—Debra May Himes

ABOVE LEFT: Arches were an important detail to soften the large footprint and expansive ceiling of this Santa Barbara style-home in the southeast part of the Phoenix metro area. The dining room is a formal yet accessible gathering place, where the cobalt-blue inlay tile under the table reinforces the elegance of the space. A custom, hand-painted Mexican tile design motif borders the floor and is referenced throughout the space.

ABOVE RIGHT: The remarkable art of the polished travertine flooring continues into the living area, where the cobalt-blue tile reemerges to create a transition from the kitchen. Likewise, the wood-paneled archway was custom-designed and provides a beautifully commanding gateway between the two spaces.

FACING PAGE: Attention-grabbing details, when used properly with contrasting elements, foster interest and intimacy in a space. Such is the case in this richly warm powder bath in a northern Arizona mountain retreat that features a copper sink cabinet with shatter glass accents, designed by Debra. A glass artist created the sink bowl. The feature wall of the bathroom is clad in black angular slate rock detail with copper and slate banding framing the mirror. The other walls and ceiling are finished in red and copper Venetian plaster to complete the dimensional radiance of the space.

Photographs courtesy of Debra May Himes Interior Design & Associates

"Being a part of the building process and watching something wonderful develop that I helped to create is beyond joyful and exhilarating."

—Debra May Himes

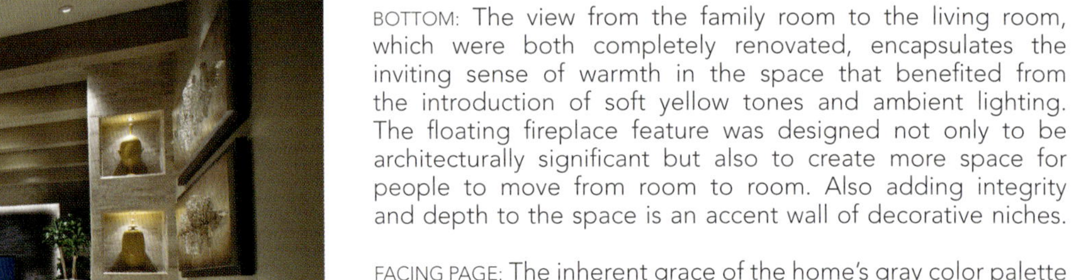

TOP: The master bathroom of a 3,000-square-foot remodel project in North Scottsdale reflects the updated look that the homeowner wanted to create throughout the entire home. A color scheme with neutral gray undertones emphasized the sleek modernity of the renovated space.

CENTER: Fully gutted and remodeled, the kitchen transformed into the homeowner's dream with new appliances and cabinets—and more storage space. The island was moved closer to the family room, allowing for more workspace and a greater sense of connectivity to the rest of the home. The granite in the island is lit from underneath, creating a romantic and soft ambiance.

BOTTOM: The view from the family room to the living room, which were both completely renovated, encapsulates the inviting sense of warmth in the space that benefited from the introduction of soft yellow tones and ambient lighting. The floating fireplace feature was designed not only to be architecturally significant but also to create more space for people to move from room to room. Also adding integrity and depth to the space is an accent wall of decorative niches.

FACING PAGE: The inherent grace of the home's gray color palette is fully celebrated in the master bedroom, which was also fully renovated. Monochromatic in spirit but far from uninteresting, the space is a study in plush materials and eclectic textures. The headboard wall features wood panels, upholstered with the back side of leather and installed in an overlapping pattern for added visual interest. The wallpaper further elevates the textural effect while providing an eye-catching backdrop for pendant lights. Debra designed the wall-hung nightstands and the bed was custom-upholstered to merge seamlessly into the sophisticated room.

Photographs courtesy of Debra May Himes Interior Design & Associates

DEMETRIOU ARCHITECTS

KIRKLAND, WA

Growing up in Cyprus, Vassos Demetriou, AIA, designed sets for school plays, not knowing how that experience would inform his chosen profession. In his late teens, he discovered architecture and began plotting a career that led him to the University of Oregon, where he earned a B.Arch., and where he currently serves as a member of the board of advisors for the School of Architecture and Allied Arts.

In 1978, Vassos founded Demetriou Architects, and ever since, the firm's focus has been design, as all architectural styles stem from good design. Vassos and his team actively listen to clients and ask questions to draw out and capture the essence of their thinking. With imagination and experience, the firm defines the aesthetic and functional requirements to deliver solutions that are distinctive and individual.

Vassos derives inspiration by creating and tailoring structures for someone specific. The relationship aspect of the design process drives him from the first meeting until the structure is complete. Building connections helps him craft a program for his clients' needs, desires, and lifestyles. He takes into consideration the functional aspects of architecture, as well as the artistic component.

With the belief that good architecture can exist in any style, as long as solid design principles are executed, Vassos approaches each project with an open mind, free of stylistic preconceptions. In the end, clients receive classic architecture that transcends time.

"My work is a process. I listen to the client and then start from the beginning without preconceptions about styling. I love to see what evolves."

—Vassos Demetriou

TOP LEFT: Vassos enjoys being involved in all aspects of design to assure a cohesive look. All of the furnishings in this home were designed and/or selected by Demetriou Architects.
Photograph by Rishel Photography

BOTTOM LEFT: Botticino fiorito marble tiles blend with a staircase of Brazilian cherry for a luxurious result. The railing of the staircase is a combination of custom finished steel and Brazilian cherry that echoes the horizontal lines in the structure.
Photograph by Rishel Photography

FACING PAGE: Located on San Juan Island, the retreat incorporates stained clear cedar siding and soffits, as well as exposed cast-in-place concrete and Corten steel panels. Materials run from the inside to the outside of the structure, resulting in a seamless composition. Restoring the property's native vegetation further enhanced the home's stunning ocean view and respect for indigenous landscape.
Photograph by Mike Jensen

PREVIOUS PAGES: True stucco walls, slate veneer stone punctuated with bronze metal beams and caps seamlessly work with Efco curtain walls and Fleetwood storefront windows to bring this residence to life. Floored in custom-colored cast-in-place concrete, the deck of the infinity edge pool features a linear waterfall, reiterating the crispness of the structure.
Photograph by Rishel Photography

"The part of the design process that drives me is the relationship, creating something for someone."

—Vassos Demetriou

TOP: Brazilian cherry floors, fir window frames, and cedar ceilings create a warm, yet rich atmosphere that perfectly blends into the vernacular of San Juan Island. The fireplace features a cast-in-place hearth with precast panels and a custom Corten metal mantel that was aged and sealed to protect its lush patina.
Photograph by Adam Behringer

MIDDLE: The Bellevue home's Brazilian cherry staircase features parallel rails that are strategically shaped so that the structure appears different from various angles, resulting in a sculptural effect. The home's exterior exhibits materials such as Raja Red slate tile, stucco, Kawneer Windows, cast concrete pavers, and steel to present a clean and cohesive design.
Photograph by Gregg Krogstad, Krogstad Photography

BOTTOM & FACING PAGE: The spaces throughout the home are organized around a courtyard punctuated with a pool. Lift and slide doors allow the area to evolve into an outdoor space effortlessly. A path between water ponds on the other side of the pool conjures the feeling of a bridge, further enhancing the outdoor atmosphere.
Photographs by Gregg Krogstad, Krogstad Photography

ABOVE: The Shore Residence sits on a small peninsula with the ocean to one side and a wetland reserve to the other. The transparency of the spaces maximizes the opportunity for views of both from a variety of locations.

FACING PAGE TOP: Demetriou Architects selected all of the furnishings for the 2,959-square-foot home. Each piece and detail is meticulously curated to bring the architectural vision of the home to life. Cork floor tiles and Vertical Grain Fir woodwork and trim further warm the space, as they beautifully blend with the Clear Cedar ceiling.

FACING PAGE BOTTOM: Clear Cedar siding combined with painted HardiePanel and an abundance of glass reinforce the horizontal lines of the home's design. The lush green space seamlessly connects to the structure, blurring the line between the interior and the exterior.
Photographs by Vassos Demetriou

"We work with clients throughout the design process to communicate aesthetic concept and vision. Through close collaboration we achieve successful results together."
—Vassos Demetriou

ABOVE: The Glass Box House is designed to respect its natural surroundings without trying to blend in. It sits atop a bare rock that drops sharply into the ocean; a manmade element that allows the nature under, as well as around it, to be preserved and enjoyed.

FACING PAGE TOP: The exterior components (exposed concrete, a glass curtain wall and Clear Cedar siding) echo each other with straight lines and squares throughout the design. The natural elements of the site provide a lush contrast to the structure, ensuring that it stands as a beacon of design.

FACING PAGE BOTTOM: The three-story glass wall facing the ocean is uninterrupted by floor plates maximizing the view of the ocean. These elements give the illusion of being outside while being inside, a treat for the senses that never gets old.
Photographs by Jay Goodrich

FENTRESS ARCHITECTS

DENVER, CO

Architecture is more than design and construction; it is an opportunity to express one's traditions and aspirations, while offering beauty, functionality and warmth to all who enter. Allowing the local culture to guide a building's design is just one of the touchstones created by Curtis Fentress, FAIA, RIBA, founder of Fentress Architects. With studios in Denver, Los Angeles, San Francisco, Washington, D.C., London, and Shanghai, Fentress Architects has been creating architectural landmarks since its founding in 1980, when Mr. Fentress brought his experience gained while working with I.M. Pei and Kohn Pedersen Fox of New York to the Mile High City. Today the firm is comprised of a team of 150 professionals who specialize in large scale, complex architecture and design.

The Fentress team believes that a building can set the tone for a visitor's experience regardless of the form the structure takes. Fentress reveals the natural order of a site and design, allowing its use to be shaped in part by the people who use it. Each plan is contextually relevant and innovative, captivating the senses to create a memorable experience. Focused, clear communication and a collaborative spirit drive the firm and have led to its spectacular and award-winning designs throughout the US and beyond, including the 2010 Thomas Jefferson Award, AIA's highest honor conferred in public architecture.

ABOVE: The "flat in the sky" includes two very large terraces that are intentionally decorated with outdoor furniture that doesn't obscure the view. The piano room includes luxurious faux fur draperies to help with sound attenuation in a room clad in hard surfaces. Built-in storage houses piano books and a platform stretches below the big screen television mounted on the wall for a sleek overall look. The three seat red "sofa" is a Fentress/McCoy original design called the Place Chair and is featured in different airports around the globe.

RIGHT: The master bathroom is a true sanctuary where the owners can find a peaceful retreat from busy everyday life. Double doors with inlaid white onyx add a natural element to the space, and when open, the stand-alone tub is allowed to take center stage, placed intentionally in line with the bottom of the window.

FACING PAGE: Wrapped in glass on two sides, the bedroom boasts a view of the mountains and one of the city skyline. The bed floats under a white lacquered frame to maximize these views. Recessed lighting above and an original Carlo Moretti chandelier offer overhead lighting, while reading lights mounted on moveable arms provide task lighting on either side of the bed.

PREVIOUS PAGES: Light grey and white marble come together in a herringbone pattern for the kitchen floor. The island, which spans 21 feet long and four feet wide, is perfect for public and private usage. A glossy hand-lacquered white "portal" serves to separate the space between the kitchen and the piano room beyond.
Photographs by Astula Inc/Raul Garcia

"It's in the details that the soul of a minimalist space speaks volumes."
—Agatha Kessler

TOP RIGHT: The dining space sits directly across from the sleek kitchen. Lights wrapped around the columns transform the load-bearing structures into art pieces as different shadows create interesting texture. A back-painted glass fireplace transforms into a conversation piece when artistic guests are invited over; a dry erase marker allows for fun—and temporary—creative expression.

BOTTOM RIGHT: Swing doors open to reveal pantry space and a fluorescent orange bar in the kitchen. When opened, the bar gives the room a jolt of creative personality against the white Italian lacquered cabinetry.
Photographs by Astula Inc/Raul Garcia

"Architecture provides a way to express regional culture in a meaningful and memorable way."

—Agatha Kessler

ABOVE: When designing the Colorado Convention Center, Fentress juxtaposed the city's vertical skyscrapers with a striking horizontal gesture: A 660-foot-long roofline that creates a memorable identity. In the process, the design also reinvented Denver's skyline, which had been static for almost 20 years. An 800-foot-long glass curtainwall offers visitors panoramic views of the Rocky Mountains and downtown Denver. Lawrence Argent's "Blue Bear" serves as an iconic gathering place for visitors.
Photograph by Scott Dressel-Martin

FACING PAGE TOP: Two layers of Teflon-covered fabric comprise the peaks of Denver International Airport's iconic roof. The sustainable airport honors local culture and geography; and the peaks represent the Rocky Mountains or Native American teepees. In designing something so memorable, Fentress turned the building "upside down" placing the mechanical systems at grade level and leaving the roof fully expressive, light and airy.
Photograph by Ellen Jaskol

FACING PAGE BOTTOM: The new Tom Bradley International Terminal at LAX was designed to emulate the waves of the Pacific Ocean. The large and small waves shield the LEED Gold Certified terminal from the harsh southern sunlight. Large-scale LED integrated media entertains and informs travelers. At the time of its completion, the airport had the most jet bridges of any airport to accommodate the superjumbo Boeing 787 and A380 Airbus planes.
Photograph by Lawerence Anderson

430

GELOTTE HOMMAS ARCHITECTURE

BELLEVUE, WA

Behind every home designed by Gelotte Hommas Architecture there are the principles that guide the firm. Creating habitable art requires an ever-listening ear to discover the client's unique perception of what "home" means to them, and utilizing an artistic eye to evaluate proper scale, proportion and composition. As principal and owner, Scott Hommas feels that design isn't as much about a "style" as it is a method and approach to architecture. Consequently, the firm's impressive portfolio includes homes that range from traditional to contemporary, from rustic to sophisticated, each influenced by the site and clients. Each home is designed and crafted using appropriate materials, textures and colors. It is this attention to detail and the flow of spaces that make a Gelotte Hommas home feel incredibly inviting. From initial feasibility studies that evaluate the merits and limitations of a potential site to a finished home, the team provides overall project guidance and employs a full spectrum of talents, skills, tools, and imagination to create a client-centered, full service experience.

Consistency of concept is also key for the Gelotte Hommas team, ensuring the home—whether it is new construction or a remodel—is true to the design theme. This is why a Mediterranean Style home feels like it could be located in southern Europe and a contemporary home bathes you in a rich but simple materiality. This standard allows clients to feel confident that their vision will find fruition in a home that is a reflection of their unique and individual personalities.

"Find a theme and stick with it if you want to build an authentic home."

—Scott Hommas

TOP LEFT: A solid antique stone bathtub imported from Europe is the crown jewel of the master bathroom. Venetian plaster, bespoke antiques, and exquisite finishes create a luxurious beauty that evokes the Old World while encouraging rest and rejuvenation.
Photograph by Ben Benshneider

BOTTOM LEFT: Hand selected stone slabs on the fireplace become the focal point of the contemporary living room. The room is imbued with rich materials throughout and simple yet elegant lighting that combine to create an ambiance perfect for gatherings of friends and family.
Photograph by Ben Benshneider

FACING PAGE: For a San Juan Islands home situated on a promontory overlooking the Strait of Juan de Fuca, the master bathroom is designed utilizing strong expressions of materials, shelter and light. The room combines all the elements necessary to wrap the occupants in luxury and comfort, much like the experience of relaxing in an exquisite resort spa. Open to the master bedroom, the story-and-a-half bathroom includes ample windows, exposed fir beams and rafters and rich stone slabs that are hallmarks of the northwest contemporary home.
Photograph by Mike Siedle

PREVIOUS PAGES: The homeowner of the Tuscan inspired whole-house remodel made a very clear request: authenticity throughout. Absolutely everything that went into the design was meant to evoke a Tuscan estate home, lovingly cared for and improved through the generations. A variety of crafts people from all over the world were employed to fully implement the design. Exterior walls finished with specialized plaster, hand-carved stone columns and trim, custom metal railings, exquisite reclaimed terracotta flooring and roof tiles and numerous antiques fill the home and delight the senses. All these design features work together to fully evoke the warmth and beauty of an authentic Tuscan-themed home.
Photograph by Ben Benschneider

"Celebrate a home's natural setting but always create warmth, so it's a refuge from the elements."
—Scott Hommas

TOP RIGHT: The impressive entry to a contemporary waterfront home welcomes visitors with a cantilevered entry canopy and views through the house to the lake beyond. Stone was selected as the primary exterior material for its inherent beauty and enduring quality. The deep accent color of the eaves and windows underscores the beautiful simplicity of the design. Like the Shaker philosophy of including only what is necessary, and that whatever is necessary must be beautiful, the home celebrates simple sophistication done well.
Photograph by John Granen

BOTTOM RIGHT & FACING PAGE: The owners of the rustic home had lived on the property for some time and found inspiration from the Pacific Northwest forest that surrounds the property. Informed by this, logs and exposed timbers are used throughout. The exposed logs in the design were hand-selected by members of the team for specific placement within the home to maximize each log's unique beauty. The home is lovingly referred to as "Cedar Haven," and many of the design details in the house are intended to evoke the experience of living under a grove of cedars. The fireplace—while "not quite large enough to roast an ox in" as the owner jokingly requested—creates a stunning focal point for conversations with friends and family around the fire. As in nature, nothing in the home is symmetrical, but is organic, elemental and reflective of the natural beauty of the area.
Photographs by Ben Benschneider

8545

IS ARCHITECTURE

LA JOLLA, CA

At its heart, architecture is about people: the people who live in a home and the people who create the architectural manifestation of homeowners' dreams. IS Architecture operates on the primary tenets of designing homes that are built to "human scale"—that is, homes that are built to be comfortable and warm no matter their size—homes that are built to the owners' lifestyle, and homes that are built to last. As one of a very limited number of Fellows of the American Institute of Architects, Ione R. Stiegler, founder of IS Architecture, leads a team of professionals who place the lifestyles of homeowners first when designing and building a home.

Whether partnering with clients to design a newly constructed home or to remodel an existing space, the team at IS Architecture views their job as just that: a partnership with homeowners. Rather than assembling a laundry list of features, the studio works with clients to understand things like where they tend to enter with an armful of groceries, if they have any special hobbies, or if they need a workspace in the home. Award-winning project managers, historic preservation specialists, and architectural historians, among others, are on hand to assist each step of the way. As Ione says, IS Architecture does everything. What that means, is the firm works for the homeowner to design a beautiful residence that feels as if it has been their home for years.

"When I hear from a client how much they are enjoying their new home, how their home feels so warm, fits their lifestyle, and feels like they have always lived there, then I know we've successfully served them."

—Ione R. Stiegler

ABOVE LEFT & PREVIOUS PAGES: The Hamptons-style home in San Diego was completely transformed from its original one-story ranch design to its current two-story design. The original structure took up too much space on the lot, depriving the owners of a usable backyard. They also wanted to install a pool, so the team worked closely with the owner—a fellow historic preservation specialist—to move key rooms up to the second floor. Exterior architectural details like stained cedar shingles and custom painted woodwork outside emulate a traditional Hamptons style. Inside, historical millwork techniques were used to create a stunning staircase with three windows that swing open to let the breeze in on pleasant days.

ABOVE RIGHT: It's the details that convey the historical style of a home. Large built-in bookcases, stately casings, and a stunning coffered ceiling complement the owner's love of color and the natural light that floods the family room. Sitting adjacent to the craft room, which may be closed off from the rest of the house by a set of pocket French doors, the family room is a beautiful example of the effect of historically-correct millwork on a room's design.

FACING PAGE: A Carrara marble island takes center stage in the kitchen, where a vaulted ceiling, complete with skylights, adds architectural interest overhead. Custom cabinetry conceals appliances in the kitchen, and a long farmhouse sink is positioned under the window to allow the owners to watch their children play in the new backyard. The adjacent breakfast area includes a built-in cabinet specifically designed to house the owners' extensive milk glass collection. When combined with the seating at the bar, the breakfast area grants the family plenty of open space for homework and family meals.

Photographs by Larny J. Mack

ABOVE: A 1910 Craftsman home in the Mission Hills neighborhood of San Diego received a new lease on life through an extensive renovation. Situated on a small lot along a heavily tree-lined street, askew from its lot lines, the house posed challenges in both expanding the footprint and creating outdoor living spaces. The team maintained the structure's original charm while meeting the owner's needs, by minimally expanding the first floor along one side and reconfiguring existing rooms to create new space for a larger kitchen, family room, and stair hall leading to the new second floor.

FACING PAGE TOP: After the remodel, the family room's stained oak cabinetry houses the home's media equipment, while the speakers are cleverly hidden behind bronze mesh cabinet doors. The wood mantel and surround of the fireplace is an original Arts-and-Crafts antique from England and melds effortlessly into the room. To each side of the fireplace, stained wood French doors lead out to the small trellis-covered patio in the side yard. The owner's collection of historically accurate furniture and accessories enhance the space.

FACING PAGE BOTTOM: Natural earth tone finishes throughout the kitchen create a warm environment that flows throughout the space. White-painted Shaker-style cabinets are complemented by the deep stained, quarter-sawn oak island designed to resemble Shaker-style furniture. The upper cabinets are adorned with backlit opaque glass panels that further emphasize the light and airiness of the room. A handcrafted copper hood and intricate tile backsplash create a strong focal point in the room. No longer compartmentalized, the kitchen now opens to a new family room. The two spaces are articulated by white-painted battered columns and flat casing complementing the existing columns in the entryway and living room.

Photographs by Larny J. Mack

JLF DESIGN BUILD

BOZEMAN, MT

JLF Design Build designs extraordinary buildings that reflect the power of the landscape around them. For more than three decades, this philosophy has positioned JLF at the forefront of modern place-based architecture in the American West and throughout the country and has fostered innovative breakthroughs that have set new standards for design-build. The team's formula is simple: they work with a small number of clients who demand exceptional design, the highest quality of craftsmanship, and timeless, distinctive building materials to set their vision apart. JLF's professionals believe that architecture is a process, not a product. Exploring ideas, giving informed advice, responsible cost estimating, discussion, discovery, and innovation are the sustaining values of architecture. JLF Design Build's projects appropriately combine cost-effectiveness with the creative process for holistic results that embrace the place.

JLF Design Build was created by the principals of JLF & Associates, a nationally recognized architecture and planning firm, and Big-D Signature, a nationally prominent construction management company. Collectively, they recognized the flaws and conflicts in traditional project delivery and sought a different way. JLF Design Build works with each client to design a structure that meets their needs, expresses their individuality, and finds a life of its own.

"Our common thread is that we all have a passion and honesty about the work. It's synergistic—everyone's craft comes together as something greater than the sum of its parts."

—Paul Bertelli

RIGHT: The beautiful form of the 19th-century stone building needs its autonomy from the entry and the rest of the home, so a glass-enclosed breezeway lightly connects the old and new masses of the Jackson, Wyoming, residence.

FACING PAGE: Authenticity of the original structure was of utmost importance during the project. Because of the harsh climate, two roofing systems are used: a technical roof complete with 21st-century techniques and a more authentic ceiling with structural purlins and rafters seen from inside. In addition, the new residence embraces original window and door openings in harmony with maximizing the views. In the living space, an original slender opening first appeared out of context, but siting the new room to focus on Grand Teton—the highest peak in the Teton Range—through the trees gives it purpose and reinforces its elegant proportion. The closer vista of the forest through the bathroom window establishes a secluded, sun-filled space.

PREVIOUS PAGES: Found miles from civilization in northern Montana, the original stone ruin was first viewed through ranch fields upon cresting a ridge, and the new location mirrors that view as much as possible. To salvage the original hand-cut craftwork and weathering pattern, each stone was numbered before being deconstructed and moved. The building's new location features blended additions that showcase the intrinsic beauty and simplicity of the stone.

Photographs by Audrey Hall

"Perfection is elusive; the joy is in the pursuit."

—Paul Bertelli

ABOVE: With a great appreciation for the design process, the homeowners were willing to revisit elements again and again until every possibility was exhausted and the design was perfect. In the master bedroom, a glass wall originally flanked the fireplace to separate the sitting room, but simplicity prompted a removal of the wall and the mantel. The result is an elegant, peaceful sanctuary.

FACING PAGE: While the exterior follows the original stone's dry stack technique with cracks and missing pieces, the inside is driven by the family's simple, contemporary tastes. Parged with mortar to add softness, the interior stone reflects the beautiful texture and exquisite materials of the furniture, fabrics, and art. Both the interior and exterior required careful selection of highly skilled craftspeople who could view a piece of material and instinctively find the beauty in its flaws. Through sensitivity to history and understanding of the materials, every piece of the home blends well together.

Photographs by Audrey Hall

LORI CARROLL & ASSOCIATES

TUCSON, AZ

Inspired by the Southwest's natural richness, Lori Carroll considers her breathtaking surrounding environment in Tucson, Arizona, one of the most vital pieces of each design puzzle. Influenced by the sublime blue skies and the mystique of the native landscape, she designs indoor and outdoor rooms with distinctive yet down-to-earth style that captures the imagination, artfully blending nature-infused colors and bold contrasts into masterpiece spaces.

Her talent, enthusiasm, and approachability, not to mention her inherent sense of vibrancy, are nearly palpable in her versatile portfolio of work completed over more than 30 years in the industry. But what is most beautiful to Lori is her team members at Lori Carroll & Associates, each of whom plays an integral role in bringing excellence to every residential or commercial project—from a charming vacation casita to a sprawling desert estate or a corporate office building. They create compelling environments that transform design dreams into reality and achieve the ultimate lifestyle for their clientele.

With a staff of accredited interior designers, computer-aided design specialists, administrative personnel, and a dedicated project manager, the firm maintains a reputation of providing the ultimate design experience. Clients benefit from the skill, consistent perspective, and combined knowledge for which the firm is known. With an uncompromising vision, a signature sophisticated-comfortable look, and endless creative ideas, Lori Carroll & Associates continues to leave an inspirational mark on Tucson and beyond.

"Nature's exhilarating elements of earth, air, fire, and water provide an enticing design palette."
—Lori Carroll

TOP LEFT: The award-winning, custom metal fire feature was designed to both blend in and stand out from the gorgeous open-air setting with minimally modern lines and a rustic-sleek finish that create a vibrantly warm focal point.

BOTTOM LEFT: Blurring the lines between indoor and outdoor living, this remarkable environment is lavished with beautiful materials, richly appointed furnishings and amenities that include a sparkling pool/spa embellished with custom glass mosaic facades flanked by captivating fire features on the perimeter. Around every corner, seating, from formal dining to in-pool lounging, awaits guests. With equal focus on indulgence and livability, this outdoor design provides the ultimate setting for entertaining.

FACING PAGE: Alfresco dining makes food deliciously vibrant and memories beautifully vivid—especially when enjoyed amidst elevated outdoor furnishings from European brand Kettal, which are sleek and sophisticated enough to be inside.

PREVIOUS PAGES: Truly the epitome of a backyard oasis, this outdoor living space reflects the inviting, southwestern lifestyle of Tucson, Arizona and is surrounded by the exhilarating elements of earth, air, fire, and water. With jaw-dropping views, enhanced with dining and lounge seating and a Jacuzzi and pool, this striking extension of the home is an incredible backdrop for relaxing and entertaining any day or night.

Photographs by William Lesch Photography

ABOVE: Nature meets style when stone, shimmering glass, and exotic wood species are expertly combined to create a bright refreshing feeling in this master retreat. With both an elegant and organic appeal, these impressive materials work together to set the tone for a soothing bathroom experience day in and day out.

RIGHT: The exterior landscape glimpsed from the master bathroom was so breathtaking that it warranted its own panoramic observation area with seating. The floating, double-sided mirror above the vanity was intentionally designed to not impact the view while maintaining the open and airy ambience.

Photographs by William Lesch Photography

"An eclectic fusion of textural tones and sophisticated materials imbues a space with warm energy and rugged refinement."

—Lori Carroll

ABOVE LEFT: The powder room in this Oro Valley, Arizona home is a lavish treat that was custom-designed with a full-length, lighted mirror in rusted metal and an attached lighted agate floating vanity. Shimmering silver leaf walls add another layer of dimension to the rich glow of the space.

ABOVE RIGHT: Curves, alcoves, and coffered ceilings are embellished with rich design elements.

FACING PAGE: A casually refined indoor kitchen maintains the integrity of Oro Valley's stunning outdoor landscapes with a ruddy, desert-inspired color palette that continues into the informal dining area. Contrasting patterns and textures from slate flooring, alder wood cabinets, patterned wall coverings, and a copper penny backsplash at once exude organic, woodsy warmth and polished modernity. The circular light fixture echoes the geometry of the architectural ceiling shapes. A hidden door next to the built-in refrigerator, both inconspicuous behind matching wood panels, provides access to a pantry that runs the full length of the kitchen—a cook's dream.

Photographs by William Lesch Photography

BITTER

"Balancing architectural and interior design elements with statement views of the outdoors brings life to every room of a home, where a mix of contemporary and indigenous pieces creates grandeur yet intimate livability."

—Lori Carroll

ABOVE LEFT: The understatedly elegant yet impactful alcove within the master bathroom needs little more than a bathtub and an incredible desert view of a rock outcropping for a simply impressive and undeniably therapeutic effect. The use of a neutral color palette, smooth stone, and richly detailed wood is naturally graceful yet decidedly opulent. And nothing is more splendid and luxuriant than a claw-foot tub, especially with the addition of the Roman-style tub filler.

ABOVE RIGHT: By utilizing exotic afromosia wood, metal, and stone this contemporary dining room becomes clean, sleek and minimalistic.

FACING PAGE: For this urban couple, resettling in a more rural location meant leaving a city high-rise behind for a spacious contemporary home at the base of a rugged mountain range. The panoramic views were inspiration for much of this home's casual, comfortable style. However, besides a natural connection to the outdoors, the clients wanted a professional chef's kitchen with plenty of room to entertain. Warm wood, the coolness of stainless and stone, along with color tones that complement this home's impressive setting are all featured here.

Photographs by William Lesch Photography

MARIA OGRYDZIAK ARCHITECTURE

DAVIS, CA

Maria Ogrydziak, AIA, founder of Maria Ogrydziak Architecture, is nationally known for her valley-inspired work and her design and policy leadership. Her bold, custom homes along with her retail and worship spaces build on 30 years in the laboratory of the California landscape. She draws from a range of inspiration including the culture of identity, the character of materials, and the region's distinct characteristics to create architecture that upliftingly transforms the everyday experience. Inspired geometries, light-filled interiors, and strong connections to the land are common threads woven throughout her structures, which often incorporate the latest green technologies as well.

Since founding her firm in 1985, Maria has designed more than 400 projects in California. Prime examples of her architectural style can be found in custom homes such as the downtown Edge Loft artist studio; the Kayak House on the American River; the Flow House in the hills of Solano; and the Flight House surrounded by agricultural fields in Yolo County.

Her retail projects include the multi-award-winning Davis Food Co-Op and Tower Records store, the Avid Reader family of independent bookstores, Newsbeat, Café Roma, and Mishka's Café. Her approach to identity and inspirational spaces has also led to numerous spiritual projects. One of her latest projects, the Glass House, is a 15,000-square-foot luxury, rural homestead with innovative green technologies and bespoke details.

"The strategic intersection of interior geometry captures exterior views and develops a one-ness between inside and outside."

—Maria Ogrydziak

ABOVE & PREVIOUS PAGES: Immersed in a lifestyle that engages with the water and the water's edge, the aptly named Kayak House is located on one of the premier kayaking rivers in northern California. Designed as a tranquil sanctuary for the homeowners to escape their busy, urban work life, the home magnificently celebrates the nature that surrounds it with a carefully planned window structure and orientation to capture the exuberance of the land and the captivating views. Building materials such as concrete floors, masonry walls, and a steel balcony and roof, were selected for permanence and solidity. The neutral color palette reflects the natural surroundings. Vertical grain fir clads the walls of the dining room and kitchen to create a golden glow—veritable reminders of the sunrise and sunset. Angled steel framing and wood window mullions suggest a texture of interior branches.

FACING PAGE TOP: A primary architectural feature of the Kayak House is the breathtaking picture window that acts as a movie screen to capture the constantly changing natural world and the riverbank outside. The view from this oversized, 18-foot-high window permeates life inside the home, as it can be seen from multiple interior spaces including the living room, kitchen, and second-floor study.

FACING PAGE BOTTOM LEFT: Stored kayaks serve as colorful sculpture pieces—and a constant reminder of river adventures just a few minutes away. When they're not in use, they hang to dry in an entry hall built of waterproof materials including a concrete floor and masonry walls.

FACING PAGE BOTTOM RIGHT: The roof deck, accessed from the second floor, acts as a private outdoor retreat overlooking the river. The popular waterway is often filled with rafters and kayakers.

Photographs by Tim Griffith

LEFT: Located minutes away from a university town in the California Central Valley, the Flight House is a rural, live/work home for a young family that sits on a 4.5-acre site. Making the most of a modest budget and an ambitious design, the home provides a clear separation of spaces along with a zero work commute and private guest quarters for long-term stays.
Photograph by Julia Ogrydziak

BELOW: The Flight House's modern, regionally inspired architectural language takes cues from the expansive valley sky, surrounding views, and circadian rhythms of the site. The signature structural wings pay homage to birds and planes and are built of an innovative TridiPanel construction.
Photograph by Julia Ogrydziak

FACING PAGE TOP: With a composition that features simple rectangles, the Flight House is a structured complex of indoor and outdoor spaces that work together to offer daylight, field views, and fresh air. The primary living space captures the diurnal cycle with east, south, and west glazing to track the sun's path from sunrise to sunset.
Photograph by Todd Quam

FACING PAGE BOTTOM: The Flight House is a statement-making 21st-century example of integrated, holistic, and sustainable design.
Photograph by Julia Ogrydziak

ABOVE: When an architect/painter and a scientist added this modern, open-ended Edge Loft to their original 100-year-old, two-story bungalow, they created an urban oasis of sorts—a place to daydream, read, paint, dine, entertain, and even host concerts. The 1,200-square-foot striped studio addition is itself an art piece, clad in alternating, colored roofing shingles. The structure references the striped buildings of medieval architecture in central and northern Italy. Similarly, colored concrete pavers create continuity from the loft to the driveway.
Photograph by Julia Ogrydziak

FACING PAGE TOP LEFT: The view from the kitchen counter in the old bungalow looks through an interior opening framed in blue stained wood. The blue color is echoed in the artwork on the Edge Loft's wall beyond, and in the sky seen through the loft window for another layer of artistic continuity.

FACING PAGE TOP RIGHT: New intersects old in this intriguing juxtaposition between the traditional bungalow and the modern Edge Loft. Former windows and doors have been made into openings to walk through or look through. Small bungalow rooms that open into the loft are transformed by being connected to the 20-foot tall volume of the new space.

FACING PAGE BOTTOM: The tall white walls of the Edge Loft are designed with carefully framed tree and sky views, alternating with stretches of solid backdrop for the homeowners' constantly rotating artwork. Visible vertical structural steel members and exposed steel-web ceiling trusses enrich the interior.
Photographs by Jay Graham

"The artistic fusion between new and old, modern and traditional, creates a compelling visual playground."

—Maria Ogrydziak

MARMOL RADZINER

LOS ANGELES, CA

Reflecting the spirit of California modernism, Marmol Radziner adopts a 360-degree approach to each project, truly designing from the big, overarching idea down to the very smallest detail—always with an eye towards strengthening the connection to nature in every design choice. Founded in 1989 by Leo Marmol, FAIA, and Ron Radziner, FAIA, the full-service architectural firm realizes their vision both coherently and elegantly through a collaborative process that integrates all elements of design.

While the team at Marmol Radziner are architects first, they also are skilled in interior, landscape, and furniture design; plus, they operate their own custom cabinet and metal shop and provide construction services in a design-build capacity. In fact, one of the most compelling aspects of the firm is that they act as both architect and contractor, providing a single source of responsibility—and a strict level of excellence—from project conception to completion. For them, it's quite simple: Good design improves people's lives—and they want to be there every step of the way.

LEFT: Located on a lush lot in the foothills of the Santa Ynez Mountains in Montecito, California, the Lilac Drive residence is nestled into a grove of existing coast live oaks, the preservation of which informed the modern, organic shape of the house. It seems as if the 3,600-square-foot contemporary residence has always existed within the established landscape, creating something of a striking visual paradox. Expansive picture windows act as frames to the surrounding views, reflecting a celebration of an indoor-outdoor lifestyle. Intersecting roof planes and deep overhangs likewise emphasize a natural sensibility with green, meadow grass roofs accentuating the second story.
Photograph by Joe Fletcher

"Architecture can be used to bring people closer to nature, extending daily living into the beauty of the surrounding landscape."

—Ron Radziner

ABOVE LEFT: The home is composed of a variety of natural materials including the Santa Barbara sandstone along with smooth-troweled, dark finished cement plaster and reclaimed wood planks. Often these materials extend from inside to the outside, as seen in the walkway to the front foyer, further blurring the boundary between the interior and the exterior.

ABOVE RIGHT: The statement staircase is a sleek addition to the residence, fusing sleek steel construction with natural oak treads that subtly reference the trees outside.

FACING PAGE TOP: The front foyer introduces the residence with a cool, midcentury modern aesthetic, popped by colorful artwork. Marmol Radziner acted as architect, landscape architect, interior designer, and general contractor for this project, fully orchestrating all of the components to work in complete harmony.

FACING PAGE BOTTOM: The local Santa Barbara sandstone fireplace wall in the living room provides an earthy counterpoint to the warm, vibrancy of the interiors, which were so important to the homeowners; the home is their sunny escape from cold Midwestern winters. A custom sofa pairs with vintage furnishings and other contemporary pieces for a multi-layered approach that adds character and depth to the space. A wall of windows and a sliding glass door overlooks the grounds and swimming pool.

Photographs by Joe Fletcher

OPTIMA

SCOTTSDALE, AZ

The result of an artist's pursuit of perfection, Optima serves as developer, architect, designer, and general contractor on every one if its projects. This unique approach to place-making allows founder David Hovey, FAIA, to ensure total quality at every step. The perfect site is chosen, views are maximized, the exterior and interior are thoughtfully designed for aesthetic and functionality, and the project strikes the delicate balance between innovative and timeless. Even before the planning begins, David is at the helm to effectively finance the large-scale undertaking. When the project is complete, Optima remains involved as its real estate sales, leasing, and property management staff ensure that all is well with the building and its residents. The Optima team is passionately committed to erecting buildings of the absolute highest quality.

Optima specializes in high-end multifamily dwellings that are sustainably designed and built. The firm employs a number of LEED-accredited professionals and has formed a long-term partnership with bimSCORE, an organization with a progressive approach to optimizing functional and business performance.

While each of Optima's creations is site-specific and unique in its own right, all are united in being appropriate for the 21st century: environmentally, aesthetically, structurally, and functionally.

"A lasting legacy can be achieved by enhancing the built environment with significant housing solutions."
—David Hovey

TOP RIGHT: Optima Sonoran Village is defined by its strong geometric shapes, large expanses of glass, and flexible floorplans that suit an array of modern lifestyle requirements.

MIDDLE RIGHT: Situated in downtown Scottsdale, Arizona, Optima Sonoran Village is comprised of five residential buildings that are environmentally integrated to create a sustainable living experience.

BOTTOM RIGHT: Indoor-outdoor living is a key component of the design.

FACING PAGE: The design brilliantly marries the built and natural landscapes. Residents enjoy the conveniences of the city while feeling connected to the beauty of the desert locale.

PREVIOUS PAGES: Camelview achieved the prestigious LEED Silver certification through the specification of locally sourced, eco-sensitive, and recycled materials; energy-efficient systems and appliances; and prolific xeriscaping. Sited on 13 acres, the building features a monumental 17 acres of roof gardens, which provide a haven for wildlife, promote evaporative cooling, re-oxygenate the air, reduce dust and smog levels, reduce ambient noise, detain storm water, and thermally insulate and shield residents from the desert sun.

Photographs courtesy of Optima

RICHARD BEST ARCHITECT

BEVERLY HILLS, CA

Striving to continuously improve the human condition and respect the natural environment, Richard Best established his eponymous Los Angeles-based firm three decades ago, after receiving his master's degree from the University of California Los Angeles and apprenticing with world-renowned architect Charles W. Moore, FAIA. Specializing in sustainable architecture, design, and planning, Richard Best Architect fosters an eco-conscious philosophy that emphasizes the LEED strategy of environmental, social, and economic prosperity.

With a deep understanding of sustainability concepts and green technology, Richard Best Architect is also able to capitalize on the highest level of eco-driven planning and implementation—always with an eye towards fiscal responsibility and high aesthetics for the ultimate design-forward synergy.

The firm's architectural design process utilizes three-dimensional modeling from the outset and throughout the process, making it easy for clients to visualize the design from both the exterior and interior. CAD-generated technical plans are created during the modeling phase to describe the construction and design intent, especially for contractors' use. The firm likewise always oversees the construction process to assure clients of a correct and accurate implementation of the design.

ABOVE LEFT The home features a gracious two-story master suite, thoughtfully designed to allow views of the eucalyptus arroyo. Frameless windows provide unobstructed views to the outdoors while the dynamic angularity of the structure unobtrusively integrates into the site.
Photograph by Adriano Sarmento/James Porschen

PREVIOUS PAGES: Situated on the upper edge of a mini eucalyptus arroyo, the remodeled home in the exclusive Brentwood area of Los Angeles evolved from a quaint 2,000-square-foot English cottage—believed to have been once owned by actor Yul Brynner—into a 6,000-square-foot modern, warm, and sustainable home for a growing family and their needs. Over the course of 15 years and two major additions, each designed by Richard Best, the 1948 cottage received a new lease on life while never losing the connection to its heritage. The original, low-slung front entry and door immediately establishes a comfortable sense of scale while nodding to the new sleek aesthetic.
Photograph by Adriano Sarmento/James Porschen

ABOVE RIGHT: The modern and linear, open floor plan includes a kitchen, casual dining room, and family room, all of which extend perpendicularly from the original 1948 structure and lead out into the rear yard and down the hillside.

FACING PAGE TOP: Tapping into the character of the cottage, both of the two-story, open-plan additions—the first completed in 2000 and the second in 2015—were thoughtfully designed and executed to fit appropriately within a challenging, half-acre hillside site. Exterior materials, including natural redwood siding, reused brick veneer, and wood doors and windows, all aesthetically hint at the original 1948 structure.

FACING PAGE BOTTOM: A respect for the integrity of the site is captured in the home's various floor levels that directly respond to the slope of the landscape. The warm, modern-style design approach is fully captured in the back of the property, which includes an infinity spa and patio area.
Photographs by Carmel McFayden

"Each home design should be unique, developed expressly to meet the residents' needs."

—Richard Best

ABOVE: The master suite features an upstairs sleeping loft and is linked back to the rest of the property via a glazed hallway which provides a dual sense of connectedness and privacy. Clad in the radiant warmth of Douglas fir wood planks, the room's modern-rustic aesthetic serves to extend the soul of the original cottage into the bedroom.

FACING PAGE TOP: The remodeled spaces of the existing cottage exude a cozy yet streamlined sensibility evoked by the reuse of the original home's exposed timber framing structure, open-plan circulation, and an inventive two-sided steel fireplace which acts as a room divider between the living room and a home office.

FACING PAGE BOTTOM: The master bathroom, outfitted in mosaic stone tile, compellingly engages with the natural beauty of the outdoors via floor-to-ceiling, frameless windows. The shower, at the right of the photo, is lined with the same Corten steel used on the exterior, again bridging the interior with the exterior.

Photographs by Adriano Sarmento/James Porschen

"Sustainability is the guiding principle around which all other decisions are made—environmental, sociological, and financial."

—Richard Best

ABOVE: A long string of wood doors and windows opens to an outdoor courtyard, which was added as a central connecting point between each of the home's additions. While the beauty of the great outdoors is celebrated in every layer of the project, it is also a highly sustainable design. Energy use was reduced by employing a high-efficiency heat pump heating and cooling system, dual paned metal window and door systems, natural lighting through a Kalwall skylight, and generous exterior glazing with extensive eaves for shading, rigid roof insulation, and earthen backing.
Photograph by Carmel McFayden

FACING PAGE TOP: The balance between rustic warmth and sleek modernity is captured in the kitchen, which directly leads into a casual dining area and family room.
Photograph by Adriano Sarmento/James Porschen

FACING PAGE BOTTOM: The open framed cathedral ceiling and wood roof trusses establish a lofty feeling and a rhythm that discretely separates the open rooms from one another. Extensive use of windows and French doors connects the indoors to the outdoors and provides abundant natural lighting.
Photograph by Carmel McFayden

SANTA BARBARA ARCHITECTURE

SANTA BARBARA, CA

A native son of Santa Barbara, Robert P. Senn has an innate understanding of Southern Californian architecture. Consistently delivering impeccable, authentic design, his firm, Santa Barbara Architecture, specializes in traditional architecture including Tuscan, Spanish Colonial Revival, French, and English Country, as well as American Vernacular styles, such as Craftsman and Cape Cod. His firm also draws from classic estates of the '20s and '30s, which gave birth to the most exquisite residential architecture in Southern California.

Robert's formal education includes a bachelor's degree in environmental design at the University of Colorado and a Master of Architecture at the University of Washington in Seattle, after which he returned to Santa Barbara, where he has designed luxury estates for more than 25 years.

With a strong belief that traditional architecture is timeless, Santa Barbara Architecture honors the look and feel of traditional European homes by incorporating courtyards, loggias, thick walls, arches, beamed and vaulted ceilings, old world hardware, and antique finishes. The firm's focus is to create authentic homes and gardens that, when finished, have the look and feel of an historic property.

Authenticity is the pinnacle goal of every project, as Robert feels that it is critical for his homes to be faithful to their historical style, and they balance modern amenities and today's lifestyles.

"When designing traditional architecture, you must remain authentic in details and materials. This creates a timeless home that when fully landscaped will appear as if it's been there for a century."

—Robert P. Senn

ABOVE & PREVIOUS PAGES: Set against Montecito Peak, the custom estate celebrates the Spanish Colonial Revival style. While the home stays true to its predecessors of the 1920s, it exudes a casually elegant appeal that's perfect for entertaining family and friends. In the motor court, period-appropriate landscaping and a Cararra marble fountain further authenticate the estate.

FACING PAGE TOP: A curved trellis punctuated with imported Italian statues carved from Carrara offers premium views of the bocce ball court. The property also offers a putting green, complete with sand traps, for outdoor entertainment.

FACING PAGE BOTTOM: The expanses of glass and light on the south side of the home promotes indoor-outdoor living. The pool is intentionally set close to the main house to make it more integral to the space. The guesthouse elegantly echoes the architecture of the main structure, as it features a handmade tile roof.

Photographs courtesy of Santa Barbara Architecture

"Traveling throughout Europe to traditional architecture, farms, and towns further enhances my design process. Seeing these structures in person helps me honor the look and feel of traditional European homes."

—Robert P. Senn

ABOVE & FACING PAGE TOP: The formal dining and living areas open to the pool and terrace. Oak floors and hand-hewn wooden beams in the living room are reminiscent of those found in the great Spanish Colonial Revival estates of the 1920s and 1930s.

FACING PAGE BOTTOM LEFT: Offering an abundance of windows and French doors to showcase the ocean views, the master suite features a covered terrace, as well as a luxurious sitting area.

FACING PAGE BOTTOM RIGHT: Intricate, hand-made iron and glass doors juxtapose simple terracotta floors in the entry foyer.
Photographs courtesy of Santa Barbara Architecture

ED RUSCHA
PHOTOGRAPHER
ED RUSCHA PHOTOGRAPHER
Ed Ruscha Fifty Years of Painting
AMERICAN CENTURY

TOMMY CHAMBERS INTERIORS

LOS ANGELES, CA

Known for his reflective, innovative twist on the expected, Los Angeles-based interior designer Tommy Chambers designs a space with nothing short of a magic touch. The delightfully unpredictable runs rampant through his work, imparting sparkling charm and wit while still aligning with each homeowner's vision.

"My inspiration comes from the client," Tommy says. "Every single project is completely unique and one-of-a-kind; that's what excites me the most about the design process." While a Tommy Chambers Interiors room may not have one signature "designer" look, what it does have is good design sense—in spades—not to mention a sophisticatedly eclectic and vibrantly whimsical sensibility.

The designer launched his eponymous firm in 2001 after eight years at Chambers and Murray as head of the interiors department and the senior business and operations manager. Putting his architecture degree to good use, he takes a classical approach to design, carefully balancing elements such as proportion and scale with the architectural integrity of the space and the client's tastes and definitions of personal comfort. His love of architecture is likewise one of the reasons why he specializes in historic restorations, especially Spanish Revival and Spanish Colonial homes.

No matter how big or small the assignment, Tommy is directly involved in every project to ensure each client receives dedicated and focused attention. Cost effectiveness and maintaining a budget is also an integral part of Tommy's work, and he is a master of the high-low design approach, seamlessly offering more accessible furnishing and décor options as needed. It's no wonder then that every single Tommy Chambers Interiors client is a referral. While Tommy and his team primarily work in Southern California, they have projects throughout the United States and abroad, where they blaze their dynamic design trail and give each room a story of its own.

"Each and every space is a background for our lives to play out, so finding the balance between formality, function, and fun is key."

—Tommy Chambers

ABOVE: Sometimes the most subtle design choices make the biggest impact. Such is the case in this Pasadena, California kitchen, which was completely renovated to create a welcoming and family-friendly environment. Melding Old World appeal with the ease of modern amenities, the space appropriately looks as if it has always been a part of the Mediterranean home—right down to the slightly antiqued, faux finish cabinets.

FACING PAGE: Originally decorated in dated shades of pink, the library in a Pasadena, California, home received a handsomely elegant overhaul, beginning with the addition of an antique marble fireplace surround and an antique Italian golden gesso mirror—both of which provide an inspiring centerpiece to the space. While it took more than two months to restore the room's wood paneling from its previously painted past, the richness of the enveloping walls were a warm reward. The four-chair circular pit is an inviting place for conversation over cigars and after-dinner drinks.

PREVIOUS PAGES: A delightful aura of playful sophistication dominates the living room for a family of four who wanted a new, lighthearted touch for their West Coast home, which was rebuilt after suffering a California earthquake. The sleek contemporary profile of a Christian Liaigre sofa and a range of moveable chairs, including a Tommy Chambers-designed bamboo piece, creates an inviting, flexible floor plan. Centered by a geometrically lively Wendell Castle coffee table, the space is not short on whimsical pizazz and a controlled use of color with the addition of a multihued, striped Paul Smith rug, "yummy" textural pillows, and eclectic art, which all enhance the warm, collected nature of the room.

Photographs courtesy of Tommy Chambers Interiors

ABOVE: Unifying Old World craftsmanship with traditional detailing affords a graciously elegant yet comfortable environment in the formal dining room. Located in a renovated 1928 Mediterranean estate, the newly constructed space elegantly balances fine antiques, including the dramatic Italian, wood-carved chandelier, with the more modest round dining table that expands to accommodate additional guests as needed. Wall alcoves likewise create a sense of depth and presence, enriching the overall composition of the room while utilizing unwanted corner space.

LEFT: The layered, livable look in the master bedroom is made for long mornings and breakfast in bed, which is perfect given that the rustic Mediterranean beach property in Ventura County is a getaway home for a busy Brentwood, California, family. The headboard is crafted from an antique bench, creating an appropriately accessible, seaside vibe, while a curated collection of tribal masks from the homeowners' travels to Africa and beyond adds a personalized, eclectic touch.

FACING PAGE: An addition to a 1935 Mediterranean house in Hollywood Hills West, California the master bedroom was designed to effortlessly blend into the home's storied character while flaunting its own luxe, streamlined attitude. The cove ceiling was inspired by the existing property, but the sleek, suggestively Turkish lines of the chaise longue and the bed's bolster pillows ensure that the room is no slave to the '30s-style architecture. The intricate, antique chandelier and sconces add drama while fresh, lush fabrics and slightly mannish, playfully striped curtains finish the room with a contemporary, tastefully casual flourish.

Photographs courtesy of Tommy Chambers Interiors

ABOVE: The traditional styling of the living room in a French Normandy house in Pasadena, California, has all the formal presence of collected antiques, including an elaborate secretary and an ethnic, carved chair. Yet the space benefits from tongue-in-cheek accents, such as boldly mod pillows and a lamp crafted from a ship's chain, to diffuse its more ornate trappings. The result is a comfortably inviting room that doesn't take itself too seriously.

LEFT: The full renovation of the historic Irving Gill home on Coronado Island, California, required a good deal of historic research to restore the property to its original wonder. A nook within the living room looks straight to the beach, but the view inside isn't so bad either. Textural, worldly furnishings and colorfully patterned elements contribute plenty of layered, livable charm while maintaining the integrity of the space's architecture. The painted Tibetan cabinet alone is a bold statement that anchors the room.

Photographs courtesy of Tommy Chambers Interiors

PARKING
FIRE LANE

WATERMARK
BY THE J RIGO GROUP
CAMPBELL, CA

John Rigo solves problems so no one knows there was a problem, but his work is so much more than just engineering solutions. His company, Watermark by the J Rigo Group, Inc. designs and builds stunning pools that lead the industry, something that John himself has been doing for decades. As the builder of the first saltwater pool in the Bay Area in 1991, John was ahead of the pack and enjoyed an exclusive for about five years. Today, he's designed passive solar systems that provide efficient heating while saving owners up to 80 percent on their heating bills. Creating exclusive, one-of-a-kind designs, privacy means a lot to John.

His clients enjoy a candid account of everything that goes into their pools. John prides himself on honesty and open communication. When you've got a question about the project going on in your backyard, his company is one of the few firms around these days that allows clients to talk to the business owner directly. Having worked with the top three largest pool companies in the world, John struck out on his own when it became apparent that many companies weren't willing to take bold steps to design unique pools that push the limits. Since then, his designs showcase the ingenuity that drives his work: he's never afraid to think outside of the box and do what others have only dreamed of before.

ABOVE TOP: Everything down to the mulch used in the landscaping was selected specifically for the Bay Area home, with the environment and aesthetics in mind.

ABOVE BOTTOM: The pool's custom built arched grotto includes a loveseat behind the waterfall. It is lit by lanterns above and LED lights underwater.

LEFT: Travertine, custom glass tile, and a beach sand interior made from crushed abalone creates a welcoming pool and spa out back. The pool runs on a passive solar power system that heats the water in an exceptionally energy-efficient manner. Custom LEDs within the pool can be adjusted via remote controls at the spa and inside the house, or via an iPhone app.

PREVIOUS PAGES: Along with pool services, homeowners enjoy custom landscaping for the front yards as well. All-custom drip irrigation systems, artificial lawns, and evergreen plants make for drought-friendly landscaping.

Photographs courtesy of Watermark by the J Rigo Group, Inc.

"Just like with architecture, designing a pool requires attention to detail, balance, and correct proportions."

—John Rigo

ABOVE: Pool proportions can make or break a design and it's always best to avoid building a pool with a width that's more than half the total length of a pool. A leaner design makes for a more graceful effect overall. The long pool built along a hillside drop off required substantial structural engineering to ensure it didn't literally fall off the side of the hill, and it is heated by a passive solar power system.

FACING PAGE TOP: Specially designed urns accent the pool and are completely hands-off. Waterproofed on the inside, the urns automatically water plants when needed and include a self-draining feature that makes landscaping hassle free. They're also lit from the inside, providing an artful touch once the sun goes down.

FACING PAGE BOTTOM: Special glass tile, custom sleek waterfalls, and a passive solar system make the pool beautiful and eco-friendly. The beach interior made with custom crushed abalone adds another natural element to the pool, which is surrounded by all on-drip landscaping that requires little maintenance. The adjacent pavilion includes a barbecue and fire pit and a built-in kitchen specifically for the space.

Photographs courtesy of Watermark by the J Rigo Group, Inc.

ABOVE: Situated right on the waterway off the Pacific Ocean, this infinity-edge project required a retaining wall to be built prior to the pool's construction in the water to hold the water back while the pool was being built. After construction was completed, the retaining wall was torn down and the water came right back up to the pool's edge. While building the pool, it became apparent that water was seeping into the property and under the home. A four-foot keyway was installed under the infinity edge surge pool to solve a major underground water situation for the yard and home. The keyway stops water from seeping under the pool and home. Special steel designed to withstand the corrosive nature of sea water was used to build the pool's structure along the ocean. The infinity edge pool includes a surge pool between it and the Pacific, to ensure that even when a large group of people jumps in all at once, the water isn't wasted.

FACING PAGE TOP: The infinity edge of the pool seems to disappear into the ocean.

FACING PAGE BOTTOM: Tiled bar stools, column lighting, and a built-in kitchen with a fire pit, barbecue, and pizza oven make the pool the perfect place to hang out. The fact that the project represents the most extreme pool design possible makes the outdoor retreat all the more appealing.
Photographs courtesy of Watermark by the J Rigo Group, Inc.

WOODLEY
ARCHITECTURAL GROUP
DENVER, CO

Led by founder Michael Woodley, the design team at Woodley Architectural Group, Inc. subscribes to a variety of architectural styles, as it creates solutions based on its clients' lifestyles, while considering site constraints and neighborhood context. With more than 30 years of experience, in a vast variety of housing types, Michael has a portfolio of work spanning high-density, multi-story and high-end custom homes. His keen understanding of current construction methods translates into designs that will stand the test of time.

The group has offices in Colorado and Southern California and has worked with some of the most respected and successful builders across the United States. Michael's hands-on approach and interactive design process has established him as a highly successful, innovative architect, sought out by a wide variety of homebuilders nationwide and abroad. His passion for good design is integral to the stellar reputation and success of Woodley Architectural Group. This passion combined with his retail approach to housing has been instrumental in winning widespread industry recognition.

LEFT: A home in Castle Pines exudes a contemporary feel with its clean lines and extensive use of glass. Nestled in Colorado's evergreens, the home respects its natural environment and maintains a rustic warmth with exquisite stone detailing. The result successfully blurs the line between indoor and outdoor living.
Photograph courtesy of Woodley Architectural Group

"Our designs are not so much based on trends, as they are a response to what the homeowner is looking for."

—Michael Woodley

ABOVE: An infill project in urban Denver offers a modern, yet controlled respite from city living. The horizontal cedar detailing offers a punch of new and different, while the brick portions of the design effortlessly blend with the context of the neighborhood. The home's striking forms give it a warm curbside appeal that constantly draws admirers.

FACING PAGE: Taking a cue from mid-century modern design, a Newport Beach home combines Brazilian hardwoods with synthetic stone by Creative Minds for a fresh approach to beach living. The tone-on-tone materials offer a textural contrast that surprises as well as delights.
Photographs courtesy of Woodley Architectural Group

"We help shape the way people live in the future with our designs."
—Michael Woodley

ABOVE LEFT: One of a series of homes built on a compact lot measuring 38 by 48 feet, a San Diego home offers an efficient bang for the buck. The 2,100-square-foot home features a two-car garage, as well as every high-end luxury amenity imaginable. The teal trim gives the exterior a whimsical, yet fresh quality.

ABOVE RIGHT: Three stories interlock in the design in response to the small size of the site. While functional, the open stairway and extensive use of windows add interest to the foyer and give the home the illusion of more space.

FACING PAGE: A southern California duplex gives a nod to Eastern Seaboard architecture with its interesting rooflines, open shutters and shingle siding. Constructed on a small lot, the home's outdoor feel seamlessly blends with the landscaping to create a natural oasis of relaxation. An open outdoor room, complete with a fireplace, allows for easy entertaining throughout the year.

Photographs courtesy of Woodley Architectural Group

"By applying lessons from luxury to affordable design, and adding disciplines from lower price points to high-end, we provide designs that continue to set the standard for innovation."

—Michael Woodley

ABOVE: The open living area of a modern mountain house in Colorado promotes togetherness and entertaining. Complete with luxurious finishes, the kitchen's interior takes inspiration from the cedar bead board ceiling. Custom cabinets and a custom cooking island continue the warmth of the space. Stone columns bring the outside in, as they add the perfect amount of rustic charm to the space and balance the stone fireplace.

FACING PAGE: Interesting forms permeate the Colorado modern exterior, as the entry stairway continues the vertical line of the home's chimney. Stone columns supporting the structure echo the chimney's lines as they bring continuity to the design. The arc of the living area opens the home to the site's breathtaking views.

Photographs courtesy of Woodley Architectural Group

INDEX

THE PANACHE COLLECTION

Dream Homes Series

An Exclusive Showcase of the Finest Architects, Designers and Builders

Carolinas, Chicago, Coastal California, Colorado, Deserts, Florida, Georgia, Los Angeles, Metro New York, Michigan, Minnesota, New England, New Jersey, Northern California, Ohio & Pennsylvania, Pacific Northwest, Philadelphia, South Florida, Southwest, Tennessee, Texas, Washington, D.C., Extraordinary Homes California

Spectacular Homes Series

An Exclusive Showcase of the Finest Interior Designers

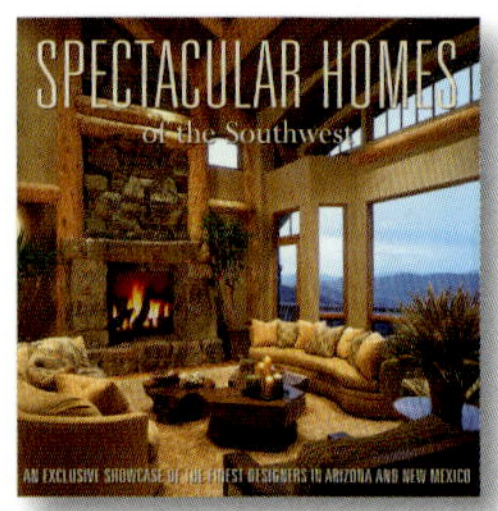

California, Carolinas, Chicago, Colorado, Florida, Georgia, Heartland, London, Michigan, Minnesota, New England, Metro New York, Ohio & Pennsylvania, Pacific Northwest, Philadelphia, South Florida, Southwest, Tennessee, Texas, Toronto, Washington, D.C., Western Canada

Perspectives on Design Series

Design Philosophies Expressed by Leading Professionals

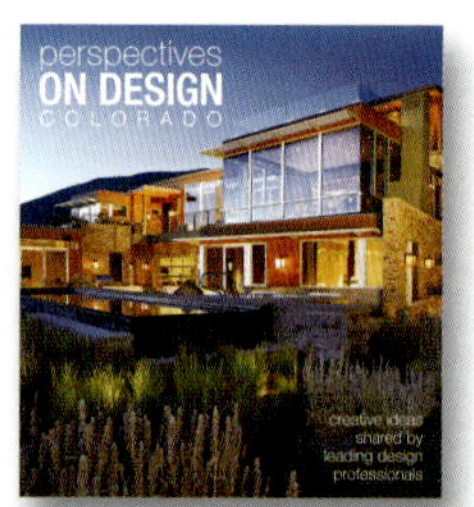

California, Carolinas, Chicago, Colorado, Florida, Georgia, Great Lakes, London, Minnesota, New England, New York, Pacific Northwest, South Florida, Southwest, Toronto, Western Canada

Art of Celebration Series

Inspiration and Ideas from Top Event Professionals

Chicago & the Greater Midwest, Colorado, Georgia, New England, New York, Northern California, South Florida, Southern California, Southwest, Washington, D.C.

City by Design Series

An Architectural Perspective by Leading Architects in the City

Atlanta, Charlotte, Chicago, Dallas, Denver, New York, Orlando, Phoenix, San Francisco, Texas

Spectacular Wineries Series

A Captivating Tour of Established, Estate and Boutique Wineries

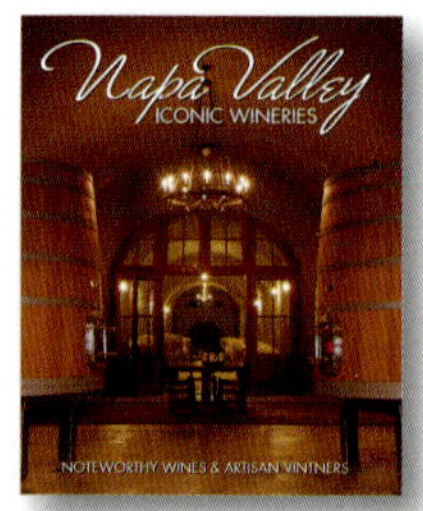

California's Central Coast, Napa Valley, New York, Ontario, Oregon, Sonoma County, Texas, Washington

Experience Series

The Most Interesting Attractions, Hotels, Restaurants, and Shops

Austin & the Hill Country, British Columbia, Thompson Okanagan

Interiors Series

Leading Designers Reveal Their Most Brilliant Spaces

Midwest, Southeast

Golf Series

The Most Scenic and Challenging Golf Holes in the State

Colorado, Ontario, Pacific Northwest, Texas, Western Canada

Weddings Series

Captivating Destinations and Exceptional Wedding Resources

Southern California, Texas

Specialty Titles

Publications about Architecture, Interior Design, Wine, and Hospitality

21st Century Homes, Distinguished Inns of North America, Into the Earth: A Wine Cave Renaissance, Luxurious Interiors, Napa Valley Iconic Wineries, Shades of Green Tennessee, Signature Homes, Spectacular Hotels, Spectacular Restaurants of Texas, Structure + Design, Visions of Design

Custom Titles

Publications by Renowned Experts and Celebrated Institutions

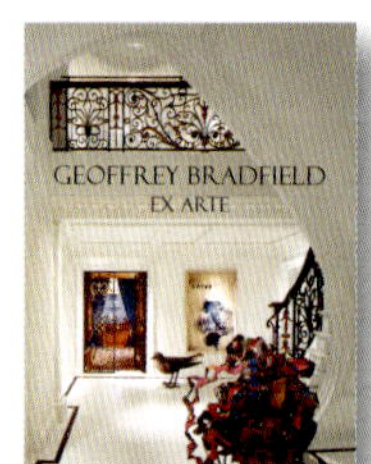

Cloth and Culture: Couture Creations of Ruth E. Funk, Colonial: The Tournament, Dolls Etcetera, Geoffrey Bradfield Ex Arte, Lake Highland Preparatory School: Celebrating 40 Years, Family Is All That Matters

Available at fine book stores (such as Barnes & Noble) and online book sellers (such as Amazon.com) or at panache.com

Panache Partners, LLC 469.246.6060 www.panache.com

Painting the Spirit Within

The Watercolors of Sibyl Sanford

Sibyl W Sanford

Painting the Spirit Within

The Watercolors of Sibyl Sanford

Foreword by Wendy Walker

This book is dedicated to my son, Philip,
whose sense of purpose, integrity and vision
are an inspiration to all who know him.

ISBN 978-0-615-20007-1

South Bay Publishing
P.O. Box 22, 1221 Harris Avenue, Bellingham, WA 98225
www.sibylsanford.com

All images in this book are for sale as fine art giclée prints. For further information,
please contact the artist at: ssanford10@comcast.net

Printing: Premier Graphics • Scanning: ArtScan • Layout: Rod Burton

Contents

SANFORD NWWS

Acknowledgments

Painting the Spirit Within came into being through the artistic and technical expertise of many people. First of all, I wish to thank my long-time friend Wendy Walker for writing the beautiful forward to this book. I am also extremely grateful for the help of Brett Baunton and Denise Snyder, who, with the utmost care, scanned each of my paintings to help produce the high-quality plates in this book. They worked countless hours to ensure that the colors were as close to the originals as possible. I greatly appreciate as well the time and dedication with which Rod Burton worked on the graphics, piecing together all of the text and plates and helping me with innumerable decisions. I am also indebted to Jessi Bergsma Rockenbach for her immense help with the final, critical touches for this book. There is no way to adequately thank these five talented individuals.

Additionally, I have been fortunate to have had the counsel of several exceptional people for editing and other advice: Peggy Kehe, who contributed great precision and expertise to the editing process; Susan Rowan, who aided with the design; Daimon Sweeney, who assisted me with the organizational format of the book; Rick Bramham, whose help with decision-making was invaluable; and Ford Hill, who provided me with ongoing support and advice.

I also wish to express my gratitude for the quality workmanship that Premier Graphics applied to the printing of this book, and particularly for the work of Tegan Cutler, who devoted much time to this project. I could not have asked for a better person to work with.

The people who formed my team while working on this book have become my good friends—and that is one of the most rewarding aspects of working on this project. My gratitude goes out to all those who helped make my dream become a reality.

Foreword

When I imagine Sibyl painting I see her garden studio with sunlight streaming in. A slender, timeless woman leans over her painting, brush intent on just the right lines, just the right spaces. The sunlight illuminates her hair and shoulders and seems to radiate down her arm and seep, glowing onto the paper and into the painting.

Sibyl and I met over thirty years ago working as wilderness rangers in the North Cascades. We shared the experience of hiking many miles with heavy loads to earn the breathtaking moments of awe and the deep peace that wilderness offers. The connection to nature we forged has only strengthened with the years. I know that it continues to enrich and inform our lives and to inspire Sibyl's art.

Sibyl paints light. At least that's how it seems to my untrained eye. She paints the light she sees and I think she also paints the light she feels.

Her paintings reflect her own inner glow and the warmth of the connections between herself and others, both human and non-human.

I have been lucky enough to share a friendship, community and bioregion with Sibyl Sanford over the last thirty years. She has brought light into my life and into our community with her art and generous, sensitive nature.

Thank you, Sibyl. Thank you for painting our daughter, capturing light streaming through her and her beloved books. (See Plate #49.) Thank you for hikes and gifts, both material and spiritual. Thank you for believing in your art, honing your skill and giving all of us the paintings and thoughts in this book.

Wendy Walker

Writer, Educator & Environmentalist

Introduction

At first glance, this may seem to be a book about watercolor painting, but actually it is a book about love. It is about love of the creative process and the colors, shapes and textures which surround us in every moment of our day. It is about love of the natural world with its infinite variety of landscapes, plants and animals; and it is about love and appreciation for the amazing people in my life, some of whose portraits grace the following pages.

This book is also about the spirit which I believe moves through all of us as well as through the forms that we see, from the tiniest blade of grass to the most massive of mountains. The forms may not be lasting, but what shines through them is. It is this sense of the inner essence of my subjects—whether they are people, Japanese cranes or flowers—that is what I most want to convey through the medium of watercolor.

To achieve this, I use pigment and water to create a quality of luminosity. My paintings almost always contain a path of light that leads from a center of interest and extends outward through the composition; but their key aspect is a sense of glow emanating from the subjects themselves—for I have found this subtle quality to be what most effectively hints at a dimension invisible to the eye.

It may be impossible to adequately express through images the feelings I have for the world which surrounds me. However, the process of attempting to do so is a constant source of inspiration and joy. My happiness derives from the journey itself, and from all the moments of aliveness that I savor—like precious gems in a long necklace. It is my greatest hope that some of these moments can be communicated, if even in a small way, through the paintings in this book.

Sibyl Sanford

The Plates

SANFORD

Part 1

Joy - Vibrancy

For me, one of the greatest joys in life is tuning in to whatever is around me in the moment. Out in nature, I love to hear the sounds, smell the smells, and touch the textures as well as to see what is before me—at such times, even the smallest things seem to take on a quality of added vibrancy and depth. Back in the studio, I relive the sensations and feelings I had while on location. It is like savoring the original experience once again, and as a result, the painting process can be tremendously uplifting.

Like the landscapes, the portraits of people and animals in this section express radiance and vitality. Some of these images arose from my response to the inner qualities of my subjects—others, from the energy of their poses. In either case, they were all painted in a spirit of joy.

*"There is no end.
There is no beginning.
There is only the
infinite passion of life."*

Federico Fellini

"May our heart's garden of awakening bloom with hundreds of flowers."

Thich Nhat Hahn

Skagit Spring
10" x 20" 2005
Plate 1

"The most beautiful thing we can experience
is the mysterious.
It is the source of all true art..."

Albert Einstein

The Azalea Path

15" x 11"   2007

Plate 2

"We are the leaves of one tree,
the drops of one sea,
the flowers of one garden."

Jean Baptiste Henri Lacordaire

Japanese Spring

21" x 29" 2007

Plate 3

SANFORD NWWS

"A thing of beauty
is a joy forever."

John Keats

Camellias #2

21" x 29" 1990

Plate 4

SANFORD

"Each moment is a place
you've never been."

Mark Strand

Garden Cascade

15" x 11"   2007

Plate 5

SANFORD NWWS '07

"If we could see the miracle
of a single flower clearly,
our whole life would change."

The Buddha

Magnolia
8" x 8" 2005
Plate 6

SANFORD

*"The capacity for delight
is the gift of paying attention."*

Julia Cameron

Tulip Time

11" x 15"   1992

Plate 7

SANFORD

"The joys of life are in the little things."

William Sanford

Tulips

15" x 22" 1995

Plate 8

SANFORD

"To send light into people's hearts,
such is the duty of the artist."

Robert Schumann

Portrait of Jeff Gilliam

13" x 17"   1995

Plate 9

SANFORD

"May you live
all the days of your life."
Jonathan Swift

Spring Fragrance
17" x 13" 1992
Plate 10

SANFORD

*"The wisdom of nature
speaks to us heart to heart,
and nature's first language
is beauty."*

Tim McNulty[1]

Water Lilies #2

11" x 14"   2005

Plate 11

SANFORD
NWWS

*"The purpose of art
is to reveal this radiance."*

Joseph Campbell

Joie de Vivre: Portrait of Monica Clark

11" x 14"   2007

Plate 12

SANFORD NWWS '07

"Study nature,
love nature,
stay close to nature.
It will never fail you."

Frank Lloyd Wright

Rhodies

21" x 29" 1994

Plate 13

"Those who bring sunshine
into the lives of others
cannot keep it from themselves."

James Barrie

Image of Mongolia: Portrait of Bolortsetseg Smith

14" x 10" 2004

Plate 14

NWWS
SANFORD

"Music is nothing
separate from me… it is me."

Ray Charles

Country Jammin': Portrait of Jimmy Murphy

12" x 16" 1993

Plate 15

"Sometimes your joy
is the source of your smile,
but sometimes your smile
can be the source of your joy."

Thich Nhat Hahn

Portrait of Celeste Cleveland

13" x 10"   1991

Plate 16

SANFORD

"One must care about a world one will never see."

Bertrand Russell

Crane Dance #2

10" x 21" 2005

Plate 17

SANFORD NWWS

*"Every natural object
is a conductor of divinity."*

John Muir

Camellias #1

15" x 22"   1990

Plate 18

SANFORD

"If you follow your bliss,
doors will open for you..."

Joseph Campbell

Rhapsody: Portrait of Jennifer Sours

13" x 14"   2006

Plate 19

SANFORD '06 NWWS

*"To me,
every cubic inch of space
is a miracle..."*

Walt Whitman

Poppies
11" x 14" 1991
Plate 20

SANFORD

"I am always doing that which I cannot do,
in order that I may learn how to do it."

Pablo Picasso

Ode to Chee

21" x 29" 2008

Plate 21

"The sun shines not on us but in us;
the river flows not past but through us..."

John Muir

Mountain Stream

10" x 8" 2005

Plate 22

Goat Lake

8" x 21" 2007

Plate 23

SANFORD NWWS

"I imagine that yes
is the only living thing."

E. E. Cummings

Crane Dance #1

10" x 8" 2005

Plate 24

SANFORD NWWS

"All seasons are beautiful
for the one who carries happiness within."

Horace Friess

Autumn Meadows

10" x 14" 2005

Plate 25

SANFORD NWWS

"We do not remember days,
we remember moments."

Caesara Pavese

Quiet Pool on Swift Creek

14" x 10"   2008

Plate 26

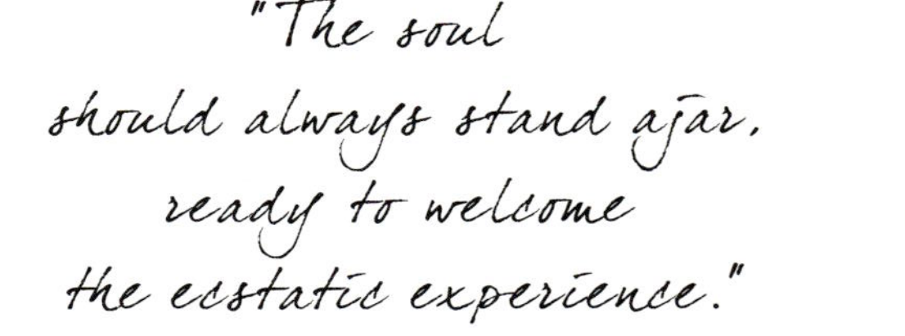

"The soul
should always stand ajar,
ready to welcome
the ecstatic experience."

Emily Dickenson

Ptarmigan Meadows

11" x 22" 2007

Plate 27

*"My soul can find
no staircase to heaven
unless it be
through earth's loveliness."*

Michelangelo

Portrait of Mt. Shuksan

8" x 13" 2007

Plate 28

SANFORD NWWS

"After silence,
that which comes nearest
to expressing the inexpressible
is music."

Aldous Huxley

Virtuosa: Portrait of Charmian Gadd

11" x 15" 1991

Plate 29

SANFORD

'02 NWWS

Part 2
Peace - Serenity

In nature, the element of water has a very soothing effect on me. One of my favorite subjects to paint is calm water with reflections—it seems to help bring me back to a deeper dimension within myself. Not only does such a scene impart a feeling of serenity, but the painting process requires it: it takes a quiet mind, great patience, and a steady hand to render the washes that create the illusion of still water.

The landscapes in this section serve as a mirror for the portraits, which are similarly reflective and contemplative.

"You cannot perceive beauty but with a serene mind."

Henry David Thoreau

"The real voyage of discovery consists
not in seeking new landscapes,
but in having new eyes."

Marcel Proust

Toward Lake Ann

22" x 30"   2004

Plate 30

SANFORD

*"The mountain
remains unmoved
at seeming defeat
by the mist."*

Rabindranath Tagore

Autumn Mist #1

13" x 19" 1999

Plate 31

SANFORD
NWWS

"Cut not the wings of your dreams,
for they are the heartbeat
and the freedom of your soul."

Flavia

Looking to the Future: Portrait of Michelle Eisinger

14" x 10" 2007

Plate 32

SANFORD
NWWS '07

*"Everything has beauty,
but not everyone sees it."*

Confucius

Canal Country

14" x 21" 1996

Plate 33

SANFORD

*"Silence
is the essential condition
of happiness."*

Heinrich Heine

Chuckanut Cove

10" x 10"   2005

Plate 34

SANFORD NWWS

"Normally
we do not so much look at things
as overlook them."

Alan Watts

Grapes
22" x 30" 1995
Plate 35

"The richness I achieve
comes from nature,
the source of my inspiration."

Claude Monet

Water Lilies #1

22" x 30" 1990

Plate 36

SANFORD

"Painting is
by nature
a luminous
language."

Robert Delauney

Yellowstone First Light

10" x 22" 2003

Plate 37

*"If you could say it in words,
there would be no reason
to paint."*

Edward Hopper

Portrait of Christina

18" x 11" 2004

Plate 38

SANFORD NWWS

*"Happiness
is the harvest
of a quiet eye."*
Austin O'Malley

View from Woodstock
11" x 22"   2005
Plate 39

SANFORD NWWS

"It is only with the heart
that one can see rightly;
what is essential
is invisible to the eye."

Antoine de Saint-Exupéry

Celesteava

12" x 8"   2005

Plate 40

SANFORD NWWS

"Come forth
into the light of things.
Let nature
be your teacher."

William Wordsworth

Afternoon Light
10" x 22"   2005
Plate 41

"Those who dwell...
among the beauties and mysteries of the earth
are never alone..."

Rachel Carson

Clark's Point

8" x 14" 2007

Plate 42

SANFORD NWWS

"We were not sent into this world
to do anything
into which we can not put
our heart."

John Ruskin

After the Dance

16" x 13"   2001

Plate 43

SANFORD NWWS

*"Trees are the earth's endless effort
to speak to the listening heaven."*

Rabindranath Tagore

Autumn Mist #2

12" x 9"   1999

Plate 44

SANFORD

*"The still mind of the sage
is the mirror of heaven and earth."*

Chuang Tzu

Alpine Reflections

18" x 30" 1996

Plate 45

"If the door
of perception
were cleansed,
everything would
be seen as it is...
infinite."

William Blake

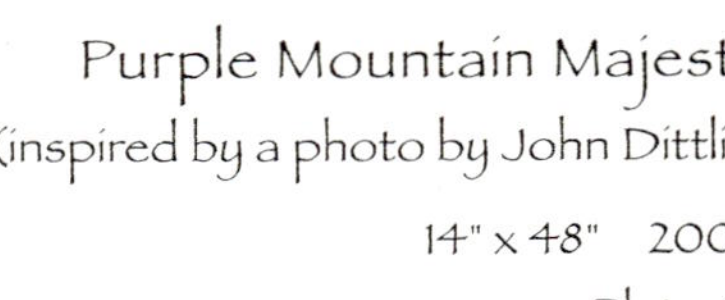

Purple Mountain Majesty
(inspired by a photo by John Dittli[2])
14" x 48"   2004
Plate 46

Room with a View

9" x 21"   1995

Plate 47

"Heaven on Earth
is a choice we must make,
not a place we must find."

Wayne Dyer

Self Portrait

12" x 17" 1996

Plate 48

ROAD TO HEAVEN
CHINESE HERMITS
SANFORD

*"Nothing can bring you peace
but yourself."*

Ralph Waldo Emerson

Erin Reading: Portrait of Erin Walcon

16" x 11" 1992

Plate 49

SANFORD

*"The personal life deeply lived
always expands into truths
beyond itself."*

Anais Nin

Etude in Black and White: Portrait of Ford Hill

13" x 17" 1991

Plate 50

SANFORD

Chuckanut Glow

12" x 28" 2000

Plate 51

SANFORD

"Although we say
that mountains belong to the country,
actually,
they belong to those who love them."

Eihei Dogen

Shuksan Sunrise

14" x 22" 2003

Plate 52

SANFORD NWWS 2001

*"Adopt
the pace
of nature."*

Ralph Waldo Emerson

Near Park Butte

11" x 16"   1996

Plate 53

SANFORD

"No matter how long your journey appears to be,
there is never more than this:
one step, one breath, one moment...
now."

Eckhart Tolle[3]

Bagley Lakes
18" x 14" 2006
Plate 54

SANFORD NWWS

*"How beautiful it is to do nothing,
and then rest afterward."*

Spanish proverb

Ladies in Waiting

16" x 28" 1996

Plate 55

SANFORD

"Who looks outside dreams.
Who looks inside awakens."

Carl Jung

Reverie: Portrait of Leslee Morrison

14" x 11" 1993

Plate 56

SANFORD

"In true art,
the formless is shining through the form."

Eckhart Tolle+

The Crane Kimono: Portrait of Christina Vu

18" x 12"   2007

Plate 57

SANFORD '07
NWWS

Evening at La Push

6" x 16" 2005

Plate 58

SANFORD

Part 3
Love - Connection

This section is devoted entirely to paintings of people and animals. Whenever I meet with someone who will be the subject for a portrait, I try to tune in to what lies below the surface, whether it is a quality of enthusiasm, gentleness, or love. I have discovered that if this is what I focus on, this is what I will see and feel. A wonderful thing happens when I paint someone. I feel a special connection to them—as if their spirit has become a part of me.

The people represented by the portraits in all three sections of this book are truly remarkable in character and presence. It was an honor to paint them.

"Love the animals,
love the plants,
love everything.
If you love everything,
you will perceive
the divine mystery in things..."

Fyodor Dostoyevsky

"A smile is a light
in the window of the soul
indicating that the heart is home."

Anonymous

Portrait of Susan Bradbury

17" x 11" 2005

Plate 59

*"The best and most beautiful things in this world
cannot be seen or even heard,
but must be felt with the heart."*

Helen Keller

The Reading Hour: Portrait of Tina and Rowell Gacad

12" x 17"   1994

Plate 60

SANFORD

*"Love the world
as yourself.
Then you can care for all things."*

Lao Tzu

What the World Needs Now: Portrait of Christina Lilleston

14" x 10" 2002

Plate 61

SANFORD '02
NWWS

"The only way
an artist can improve what he sees
is by expressing feelings."

Alvaro Castagnet[5]

Tender Moment

18" x 14" 1996

Plate 62

SANFORD

"If a thing loves,
it is infinite."

William Blake

Just Kidding

9" x 11" 1996

Plate 63

SANFORD

"The way to know life
is to love many things."

Vincent Van Gogh

Morning Greeting
22" x 30" 1996
Plate 64

SANFORD

"If you want to know me,
look inside your heart."

Lao Tzu

Portrait of Marc Chesler

14" x 11" 2001

Plate 65

SANFORD NWWS 2001

"Art is the point of contact with love."

Sufi saying

Barb and Peebers: Portrait of Barbara Twist

11" x 11" 1997

Plate 66

SANFORD

"The heart
is a thousand-stringed instrument
that can only be tuned with love."

Hafiz

Portrait of Marinette Moody

13" x 10" 2007

Plate 67

SANFORD
NWWS '07

"The love
we give away
is the only love we keep."

Barbara De Angelis

Portrait of Loan and Christina Vu

17" x 13"   1992

Plate 68

"To love and be loved
is to feel the sun from both sides."

David Viscote

Portrait of Jody and Bob Guenser

10" x 13" 2006

Plate 69

SANFORD 2006
NWWS

"There are two ways of spreading light:
to be the candle
or the mirror that reflects it."

Edith Wharton

Soul Mates: Portrait of Mandy Horowitz and Celesteava

13" x 11"   2005

Plate 70

SANFORD

*"Do not follow where the path leads.
Rather go where there is no path
and leave a trail."*

David Perkins

Graduation Day: Portrait of Philip Gerity

17" x 12"   2002

Plate 71

SANFORD '02 NWS

"Each friend
represents a world in us."

Anaís Nín

Tommy

8" x 12" 2001

Plate 72

SANFORD NWINS 2001

*"To his dog,
every man is Napoleon."*

Aldous Huxley

Portrait of Ford Hill and Kairos

9" x 13"   2002

Plate 73

SANFORD
NWWS '02

*"If you love it enough,
anything will talk with you."*

George Washington Carver

Kairos and Yola

8" x 13"   2006

Plate 74

SANFORD NWWS '06

"We are shaped and fashioned
by what we love."

Johann Wolfgang Von Goethe

Man's Best Friend: Portrait of Hal Robinson and Vanya

10" x 14" 2005

Plate 75

SANFORD NWWS

*"Sometimes the heart sees
what is invisible to the eye."*

H. Jackson Brown, Jr.

Portrait of Dash

10" x 7"   2005

Plate 76

SANFORD
NWWS 2005

*"What lies behind us and what lies before
us are tiny matters
compared to what lies within us."*

Ralph Waldo Emerson

Inseparable: Portrait of Susan Rowan and Amber

13" x 10" 2007

Plate 77

SANFORD NWWS

"Living is giving,
is loving,
is living."
William Sanford

Mystical Light: Portrait of Eileen Bowden
12" x 17"   1995
Plate 78

SANFORD

The Process

The Process

"Where the spirit
does not work with the hand,
there is no art."

Leonardo da Vinci

For me, painting is a very intuitive process. Usually my inspiration comes from an emotional response to an experience deeply felt, leaving me with a sense that an image wants to be created. From that moment, a work of art seems to take on a life of its own, dictating what it needs at every step of the way. My task is to show up in my studio every morning with a quiet, receptive mind, ready to follow directions. Because of this, I like to approach every painting from a place of "not knowing," so I can be open to whatever I am led to do in the moment. Often after I finish a painting, I find myself wondering in amazement how it happened.

And yet there are principles behind everything I do. I can say, for instance, that the secret to creating luminosity in watercolor lies in contrast—for it is the range of values (lights and darks) in a painting that provides an opportunity for dramatic light effects. To illustrate some of the principles and techniques used in my painting process, including the method for layering glazes, I have reproduced the image, "Chuckanut Glow" (Plate 51), in stages.

Step One:

After creating a value study to plan the placement of lights and darks, I drew my composition on a piece of Arches 300 lb. paper. Using a large brush, I painted three separate washes of Yellow Ochre, Rose Madder Genuine, and Cerulean Blue, allowing the paper to dry completely before applying each succeeding wash. I retained the white of the paper where I wanted the light to be brightest.

Step Two:

Beginning with the sky, I began painting the most distant areas of the picture, making sure to leave a line of light on the horizon. For the hues of the farthest islands, I used combinations of the three colors mentioned above, adding more layers of paint to achieve the proper value. With a damp brush, I softened the edges of the land forms, which allowed them to recede into the distance.

Step Three:

I added Ultramarine Blue and Cadmium Red to my palette and began to work on the middle land masses, increasing the darks as I came closer to the foreground. Within each shape, I made sure to change color several times to add interest and variety to the painting.

Step Four:

Next, I began working on the small central island, which was to be the focal area of the painting. To ensure that this area would attract the viewer's eye first, I added more intense color and detail here. At this point, I also adjusted the values of the water with additional washes to add to the feeling of glow. I then painted the shadows on the water with extreme care, so as not to disturb the underlying washes.

Step Five:

I added Winsor Blue and Alizarin Crimson to my palette and began to lay in color on the foreground. First, I painted the area that was bathed in light to emphasize the brighter hues and then gradually added darker values to the surrounding trees and hills. Here again, I repeatedly changed color, moving from warm to cool mixtures of hues.

Step Six:

Softening edges as I went, I adjusted the values of the foreground and added a few highlights to the shadow shapes by removing paint with a stiff brush. I then gave the painting a final check to make sure that the edges were varied, that the shapes differed in size, form, and texture, and that the values had enough contrast.

Now that the painting no longer indicated that it needed something more, I knew it was complete.

Index of Paintings

Joy - Vibrancy

Plate 1 – Skagit Spring, p. 18

Every spring, the Skagit Valley, just south of Bellingham, is arrayed in a spectacular display of tulips of every known description and color. This painting was an opportunity to work with vibrant color. My favorite moment was adding the splash of yellow near the horizon line.

Plate 2 – The Azalea Path, p. 21

After visiting the Portland Japanese Garden in Oregon, I painted this image of the Shade Garden because it combined the energetic magenta hues of the azalea path with a serene atmosphere. I tried to convey both feelings in this painting. (See also Plates 3 and 5.)

Plate 3 – Japanese Spring, p. 23

This scene was from another section of the Portland Japanese Garden. Here again, I felt a sense of vibrancy from the colors and yet at the same time a deep feeling of serenity from the quiet reflections in the water. The great challenge in this composition was rendering the many types of foliage and mixing the myriad shades of green. (See Plates 2 and 5.)

Plate 4 – Camellias #2, p. 25

This painting is typical of most of my floral works. It was begun with a free and abstract wash and then was slowly built up using the technique of "negative" painting—that is, painting around the forms. I learned this technique and many others in the late 1980s from my mentor, Carol Orr, a superb painter and teacher. I will always be grateful for the knowledge she imparted to me. This image was juried into the 1990 Northwest Watercolor Society Open Show.

Plate 5 – Garden Cascade, p. 27

This is the third scene from the Portland Japanese Garden. (See Plates 2 and 3.)

Plate 6 – Magnolia, p. 29

This flower was originally part of a larger painting, but I felt it made a more powerful statement on its own.

Plate 7 – Tulip Time, p. 31

The main features of this painting are its "lost and found" edges and the "Z" formation of the composition leading the eye through the picture. This painting was juried into the 1992 Northwest Watercolor Society "Waterworks" Show.

Plate 8 – Tulips, p. 33

For an explanation on technique, refer to Plate 4.

Plate 9 – Portrait of Jeff Gilliam, p. 35

My friend Jeff is a master musician and an outstanding teacher. While he is a person of great energy and passion, he also has a kind and compassionate spirit. In this portrait, I tried to create a sense of unity by connecting the figure to the background through the use of color. I carried some of the subtle background hues into the folds of the shirt and even into the dark shape of the piano.

Plate 10 – Spring Fragrance, p. 37

In this painting, I used an "S" shape to guide the viewer's eye through the picture. The figure pausing to smell the flowers is the focal point of the painting. This picture incorporates an impressionistic style, similar to that used in "Tulip Time" in Plate 7, and was painted around the same time.

Plate 11 – Water Lilies #2, p. 39

For an explanation on technique, refer to Plate 4.

Plate 12 – Joie de Vivre: Portrait of Monica Clark, p. 41

Monica, a talented musician, has a warm and fun-loving spirit. The challenge of this painting lay in choosing a harmonious background color, and it took two tries to come up with the one I wanted. Monica's friends are featured in Plates 19 and 32.

Plate 13 – Rhodies, p. 43

For a discussion on technique, see the explanation for Plate 4.

Plate 14 – Image of Mongolia: Portrait of Bolortsetseg Smith, p. 45

Although I had to make two attempts to capture Bolor's likeness, my main focus in this painting was to convey a sense of her compassionate and loving nature. Bolor was raised in the Arkhangai Province of Mongolia and is wearing a traditional dress in blue—symbolizing the sky.

Plate 15 – Country Jammin': Portrait of Jimmy Murphy, p. 47

Jimmy, a country music star, is a superb musician. This painting combines a feeling of energy, conveyed by the muted red tones, with a sense of inner peace and gentleness—reflecting Jimmy's spirit.

Plate 16 – Portrait of Celeste Cleveland, p. 49

Celeste is enormously talented. Not only is she a fine dancer, but she also plays the violin beautifully. I chose to paint her in an energetic pose and then used a golden background to enhance the feeling of joy in the picture.

Plate 17 – Crane Dance #2, p. 50

I have always loved cranes, and they are a natural subject for my Japanese series. I collected images of these magnificent birds from many sources and then carefully crafted the composition for this mating dance. (See also Plate 24.)

Plate 18 – Camellias #1, p. 53

For a discussion on technique, refer to the explanation for Plate 4.

Plate 19 – Rhapsody: Portrait of Jennifer Sours, p. 55

Jennifer, a lovely person and a very gifted musician, plays both the piano and the violin. She studied piano with Jeff Gilliam (Plate 9). In this portrait, I tried to convey a feeling of the sounds of the music through the movement of brush strokes in the background. Jennifer's friends appear in Plates 12 and 32.

Plate 20 – Poppies, p. 57

For a discussion on technique, see the explanation for Plate 4.

Plate 21 – Ode to Chee, p. 59

This painting is one of a series that I embarked on to learn how to paint koi, a fish which is common in Japanese gardens. I love these fish for their bright colors, and have studied them for years. However, they are challenging to paint, in part because the water surrounding them is difficult to render. I have dedicated this image to one of my favorite mentors, Cheng-Khee-Chee, a renowned watercolorist who is a master at painting koi.

Plate 22 – Mountain Stream, p. 61

This painting was inspired by the little creeks that gurgle through the meadows near Mt. Baker. I love to sit and listen to the melodies of these streams, for each one carries a different tune. They are magical places.

Plate 23 – Goat Lake, p. 62

While hiking along the Ptarmigan Ridge Trail in the Mt. Baker Wilderness, I saw this lake in the distance and went down a rocky ridge to inspect it more closely. What had appeared to be an easy walk turned into a strenuous detour! However, it was worth the effort, and I was rewarded by seeing twelve mountain goats on the way.

Plate 24 – Crane Dance #1, p. 65

This image of a Japanese crane was actually done as a study for the larger painting in Plate 17. I softened edges to create a feeling of movement, and added some of the background colors to the bird's white plumage. In Japan, the crane is a symbol of happiness.

Plate 25 – Autumn Meadows, p. 67

The autumn hues in the mountains of the Pacific Northwest are truly breathtaking. This scene of Heather Meadows and Picture Lake near Mt. Baker was a great excuse to use a palette of complementary colors.

Plate 26 – Quiet Pool on Swift Creek, p. 69

This image depicts a special place on the Lake Ann Trail in the Mt. Baker Wilderness, with a view of Mt. Baker in the distance. Again, I used complementary hues to capture a sense of the brilliance of this autumn day.

Plate 27 – Ptarmigan Meadows, p. 70

This painting represents a moment of indescribable elation. Sitting in this alpine meadow surrounded on all sides by autumn color was an experience that I will never forget. Here, the hues of oranges and reds are close to what I actually saw.

Plate 28 – Portrait of Mt. Shuksan, p. 73

Mt. Shuksan, in the Mt. Baker Wilderness east of Bellingham, is one of the most photographed mountains in the world. This painting is a true portrait, rendered with great attention to detail.

Plate 29 – Virtuosa: Portrait of Charmian Gadd, p. 75

I took the photos that inspired this painting when Charmian, a long-time friend, was visiting from Australia. She is the finest violinist I have ever heard, and no doubt ever will, and at that time was playing a violin made by Stradivarius. In a way, this is a portrait not only of Charmian, but of the violin as well. My main intent with this painting was to capture a feeling of rapt concentration and energy and to convey a sense of the sublime sounds of the instrument. With this in mind, I softened the top edge of the violin and allowed it to disappear into the background. This is one of the earliest portraits in the book.

Peace - Serenity

Plate 30 – Toward Lake Ann, p. 79

Over the years, I have found favorite resting spots in the mountains, and this painting was inspired by one of them. This lovely place is nestled in a valley on the way to Lake Ann, which is in the Mt. Baker Wilderness. Mt. Shuksan lies in the background shrouded in mist, helping to lead the eye through the composition.

Plate 31 – Autumn Mist #1, p. 81

I like to paint fog because it adds an air of mystery to a scene. This image of Mt. Shuksan peering through the mist over Picture Lake was on the cover of the North Cascades Institute catalogue for 2003, and also included in the book, "Whatcom Places II," published by the Whatcom Land Trust in 2007.

Plate 32 – Looking to the Future: Portrait of Michelle Eisinger, p. 83

Michelle is a beautiful person with tremendous musical talent. She studied piano with Jeff Gilliam (Plate 9). The most difficult part of this painting was determining what colors to use in the background; in the end, I used a grayer version of the same hues that I used in the figure. Her friends Monica and Jennifer are featured in Plates 12 and 19.

Plate 33 – Canal Country, p. 85

This painting was inspired by the scenery of western Skagit Valley, which is prime agricultural land dotted by canals. The "Z" formation of the canal leads the eye back through the composition to the trees and hills beyond. The main challenge in this painting was creating variety, texture and interest in the foreground grasses.

Plate 34 – Chuckanut Cove, p. 87

This painting depicts one of the many coves along Chuckanut Drive near Bellingham. To create more interest in this composition, I added fog and glowing light to the background.

Plate 35 – Grapes, p. 89

For information on technique, see the explanation for Plate 4.

Plate 36 – Water Lilies #1, p. 91

This is one of the early paintings in the book. For information on technique, see the explanation for Plate 4.

Plate 37 – Yellowstone First Light, p. 92

In 2002, I took a natural history trip to Yellowstone National Park with a group called Defenders of Wildlife for the purpose of observing bears and wolves. To see the animals we were looking for, we had to start out on our search before sunrise. This painting was created as a result of one of those early morning outings.

Plate 38 – Portrait of Christina Vu, p. 95

Christina has been my model for several paintings. (See Plates 57 and 68.) She is wonderful to work with and has a lovely, strong spirit. This painting features a palette of complementary colors. It was juried into the 2005 Northwest Watercolor Society Open Show.

Plate 39 – View from Woodstock, p. 96

This image represents an example of layering glazes to capture a sense of glow. Not only does this technique contribute to an atmosphere of tranquility, but it requires a steady hand and a quiet mind for its successful execution.

Plate 40 – Celesteava, p. 99

Celesteava, who belongs to my friend Mandy Horowitz, is not an ordinary cat—to those who know her, she has a very wise and magical spirit. In this image, I wanted to convey a sense of her essence through the use of color and light. (See also Plate 70.)

Plate 41 – Afternoon Light, p. 100

The photographs for this painting were taken in late afternoon light while the colors in the foreground were still quite vibrant. It was painted using the same layered glaze technique found in many of the paintings in this section.

Plate 42 – Clark's Point, p. 103

I visited this beautiful spot near Bellingham in the early evening, and the light that I saw took my breath away. The trees were briefly back-lit with an orange hue, and I had only a few minutes to take photos before the sun went down.

Plate 43 – After the Dance, p. 105

In 2001, I attended a watercolor workshop in Portland, Oregon, with renowned artist, Arnie Westerman, during which he took our group to a dance studio to photograph ballerinas. I painted this picture after I had returned home. This pose forms a triangular composition, which is balanced by the addition of the picture on the wall at the upper right.

Plate 44 – Autumn Mist #2, p. 107

This painting is similar to Plate 31 in its location and atmosphere and was also painted around the same time.

Plate 45 – Alpine Reflections, p. 109

To commemorate my experience as a ranger in the Glacier Peak Wilderness, I painted this scene of Image Lake with Glacier Peak looming over it—one of the great scenes of the Pacific Northwest. My friend Wendy Walker, who wrote the foreword to this book, was the ranger at Image Lake. Many years later, as I was painting this picture, I was flooded with memories from those unforgettable days of living and working in the wilderness.

Plate 46 – Purple Mountain Majesty, p. 110

This painting was inspired by an image taken by noted mountaineer and photographer John Dittli.[6] What attracted me was the magnificent light across the expanse of receding mountain ranges—something that I have often experienced and marveled at. Mt. Baker lies in the far distance with the silhouette of Mt. Shuksan in front of it.

Plate 47 – Room with a View, p. 112

One day while driving south on the interstate toward Bellingham, I glanced to the side and saw a herd of cows grazing on a hill with Mt. Baker towering in the background. I raced home, grabbed my camera, and drove back to the scene. This painting was the result, and was created by multiple layered glazes.

Plate 48 – Self Portrait, p. 115

I created this painting for a show which had as its theme "self portraits and portraits of artists." I used the same process for this picture as I do for all other portraits and had someone come to my home to take my photograph. It was rather strange painting a portrait of myself, but I kept my mind focused on shapes, colors and washes. My favorite part of the picture is the title of the book that I was reading at the time.

Plate 49 – Erin Reading: Portrait of Erin Walcon, p. 117

Erin, a Theater Arts educator, is the daughter of my friend Wendy Walker, who wrote the foreword to this book. Like her remarkable mom, Erin brings talent and brilliance to the work she does. In this early portrait, painted 16 years ago, I captured Erin doing what she has always loved—reading.

Plate 50 – Etude in Black and White: Portrait of Ford Hill, p. 119

Even though this is an early portrait, it has a special significance for me. Ford is a brilliant musician from whom I was privileged to take piano lessons in the late 70s; it was a life-changing experience for me. The remarkable thing about Ford is that, even when he plays a piece of virtuosic difficulty, he exudes an atmosphere of calm. The depth and resonance of his tone is truly amazing. More than this, Ford is one of my dearest friends. He expresses the qualities of humility, humor, and generosity in everything that he does. I am greatly blessed by his presence in my life. (See also Plate 73.)

Plate 51 – Chuckanut Glow, p. 120

This may be the most well-known of my paintings, depicting the breathtaking scenery off Chuckanut Drive near Bellingham. The techniques used in the creation of this image are explained in detail in the "The Process" section of this book. This painting is also to be the cover image for the upcoming book, "Chuckanut," by Ken Wilcox.

Plate 52 – Shuksan Sunrise, p. 123

At Artist Point near Mt. Baker, one can find several tarns, or mountain pools, reflecting the image of Mt. Shuksan. I was there one morning early enough to see the sun rise, and the scene was breathtaking. The rocky, barren landscape set off the majesty of the mountain with its intricate glacial patterns.

Plate 53 – Near Park Butte, p. 125

One summer, I hiked up several buttes surrounding Mt. Baker and created a series of paintings from these viewpoints. This picture was the only one in the series that did not feature Mt. Baker. I had followed these horses all the way up a steep trail for four miles, and I felt that at the very least they could provide me with the focal point for a painting!

Plate 54 – Bagley Lakes, p. 127

This area is another sublime, easily accessible spot in the Heather Meadows area near Mt. Baker. In this painting, I used the line of the path to help lead the eye through the picture. My aim was to raise the viewer's curiosity as to what was lying just around the corner—which was exactly what I was wondering when I hiked the trail!

Plate 55 – Ladies in Waiting, p. 129

I came across this barnyard scene in Canada while driving to Vancouver. I was immediately fascinated by the brown and white patterns on the cows and shot two rolls of film of these placid animals. This painting is mainly about shapes, but the complementary colors of blue and Burnt Sienna were also carefully chosen.

Plate 56 – Reverie: Portrait of Leslee Morrison, p. 131

My long-time friend Leslee is a teacher, counselor, healer—and an author of two books. Because she is by nature both reflective and highly intuitive, I chose to paint her in a contemplative pose for this portrait. To add to the sense of mood here, I used a limited palette of colors. This picture was juried into the 1993 Northwest Watercolor Society "Waterworks" Show.

Plate 57 – The Crane Kimono: Portrait of Christina Vu, p. 133

This is probably the most complicated painting that I have done to date. The kimono alone took at least 20 hours to paint. However, the most technically difficult part of the picture was the background, which consisted of many washes. Christina patiently posed for two separate sittings while I shot more than four rolls of film. I particularly wanted to capture Christina's inner radiance through a sense of glow, in contrast to the highly-detailed kimono. Although the color scheme of the painting is quite vibrant, it actually contains a very limited range of hues. This painting was juried into the 2008 Northwest Watercolor Society Open Show. (See also Plates 38 and 68.)

Plate 58 – Evening at La Push, p. 134

This sunset on the Olympic coast with its wonderful oranges was one of the most dramatic that I have seen in recent years. I was additionally drawn to this scene because of its simplicity and its large, dark shapes. It is one of the few compositions in the book that I did not need to alter much before painting it—this is close to what I actually saw.

Love-Connection

Plate 59 – Portrait of Susan Bradbury, p. 139

Susan is one of the most amazing people I know. She is immensely energetic, loving and compassionate. In addition to being a fine acupuncturist, she travels the world initiating peace projects in regions such as Israel, Palestine, Africa, South Korea, and Mongolia. This was a difficult portrait to paint because my reference photos were dark and because there are always challenges inherent in capturing someone smiling. I was careful to unify this painting by using a limited palette. This painting was juried into the 2006 Northwest Watercolor Society Open Show and won the Bellevue Art and Frame Award.

Plate 60 – The Reading Hour: Portrait of Tina and Rowell Gacad, p. 141

Tina and her family, originally from the Philippines, have been very close friends both to me and to my son, Philip, for many years. Tina is a very beautiful and caring person. Rowell, the youngest of her three remarkable sons, is a gifted student. This painting was juried into the 1994 Northwest Watercolor Society Open Show.

Plate 61 – What the World Needs Now: Portrait of Christina Lilleston, p. 143

Christina's mother, Martina, is a dear friend of mine, and Christina is the youngest of her three lovely daughters. I took the photograph for this painting after the September 11th attack in New York, and this image was my emotional response to that horrific event. This painting was juried into the 2003 Northwest Watercolor Society "Waterworks" Show.

Plate 62 – Tender Moment, p. 145

Some years ago, I was on the Outer Banks of North Carolina and encountered a small herd of wild ponies. I sat quietly watching them, and after a while a foal left its mother's side and walked over to me. To my great amazement and delight, he reached out and nuzzled me. It was a magical moment that I will never forget. Naturally, when I arrived home, I was very motivated to paint this image of the foal with its mother.

Plate 63 – Just Kidding, p. 147

I met these two goats at a petting zoo in Canada and sat watching them for a long time. After several rolls of film, I finally captured the image that I was waiting for when they paused momentarily during their exuberant play.

Plate 64 – Morning Greeting, p. 149

I have had a special love of horses ever since I was a child, and they are subjects that I know well. In this painting, I wanted the line of the fence to tie the composition together, and I therefore attached it to the shadows of the horses to create one larger shape. The horse on the left side, with his white markings, is the center of interest. In this picture, I tried to portray each horse as a unique individual.

Plate 65 – Portrait of Marc Chesler, p. 151

My friend Marc was a very fine acupuncturist who used to fly up to Washington from California every other week to work with patients. Sadly, he passed away in 2001. Not long afterward, I painted this portrait in his memory and gave it to his parents.

Plate 66 – Barb and Peebers: Portrait of Barbara Twist, p. 153

Barb was a wonderful friend who always had a twinkle in her eye and a terrific sense of humor. We became very close through our mutual passion for art and music. I have greatly missed her since her passing in 1997—her spirit will always be with me.

Plate 67 – Portrait of Marinette Moody, p. 155

My close friend Marinette has a beatiful heart and a warm smile, and in this portrait I wanted most of all to capture a sense of her inner radiance. To create a feeling of unity, I used a limited palette and layered the colors from the figure into the background.

Plate 68 – Portrait of Loan and Christina Vu, p. 157

This painting, completed 16 years ago, is one of the early portraits in the book. Loan, who was born in Hanoi and raised in Saigon, Vietnam, has been my friend and hairdresser for many years. Christina, her beautiful and artistically talented daughter, appears in more recent portraits in Plates 38 and 57.

Plate 69 – Portrait of Jody and Bob Guenser, p. 159

Jody and Bob's son Josh, a very good friend of my son, Philip, asked me to paint a portrait of his parents for their wedding anniversary. In this painting, I wanted to convey a sense of intimacy between these two very special people. I used soft light and lost edges to enhance this feeling.

Plate 70 – Soul Mates: Portrait of Mandy Horowitz and Celesteava, p. 161

My dear friend Mandy is the most light-filled person I know—she radiates love. She is a great blessing in my life, and I cherish her friendship. Mandy has a particularly deep connection with her cat Celesteava, and a mutual understanding flows between them. The photograph for this painting was back-lit, which was ideal for my intention to capture a strong sense of glow. (See also Plate 40.)

Plate 71 – Graduation Day: Portrait of Philip Gerity, p. 163

I painted this portrait of my son, Philip, using a photograph I took on the day of his graduation from college. Phil's presence in my life is a true gift, for he is much more than a son to me—he is a close friend. In this painting, I wanted very much to capture a sense of his kind and caring spirit. This book is lovingly dedicated to Philip.

Plate 72 – Tommy, p. 165

Tommy was my devoted companion and trusted friend for thirteen years. He was always full of life and eager to have fun, no matter what the occasion was. I painted this portrait of him after he had passed away, and as I worked on this piece I truly felt that he was there with me helping to guide the brush.

Plate 73 – Portrait of Ford Hill and Kairos, p. 167

I have never seen an animal as attached to its master as Kairos was to Ford. One would often see Kairos sitting and staring at Ford in loving devotion. Ford, in turn, was a dedicated guardian and structured his life around Kairos' needs. The challenge of this painting was to create a sense of unity between the brown tones of Kairos' fur and the rosy tones surrounding Ford. I was careful to combine both of these hues in the couch and the background to help tie them together. (See also Plates 50 and 74.)

Plate 74 – Kairos and Yola, p. 169

Ford's dogs, Kairos and Yola, combined the qualities of uncanny intelligence with the utmost devotion and loyalty. Yola will always remain in my mind as the most elegant, polite, and patient dog I have ever known, while Kairos will always be remembered as the most devoted. The challenge of this painting lay in creating a color scheme that was not too brown, so I was careful to include plenty of red, blue and purple. (See also Plate 73.)

Plate 75 – Man's Best Friend: Portrait of Hal Robinson and Vanya, p. 171

Hal, from New York City, is a long-time friend of Ford Hill. (See Plates 50 and 73.) A kind and gentle spirit, he is also a talented actor and singer and has performed in many theaters around the country. His dog, Vanya, did not want to be photographed that day, so Hal had to hug her tightly to keep her still. However, the pose worked out perfectly for my purposes.

Plate 76 – Portrait of Dash, p. 173

Dash is the beloved companion of Kathy Brown, a professional dog trainer, and is one of the most beautiful dogs I have ever seen. His eyes have great depth and a sense of soul, and I spent a considerable amount of time rendering them. After that, the painting happened very quickly. I finished by adding a rainbow of color to the shadow side of his ruff.

Plate 77 – Inseparable: Portrait of Susan Rowan and Amber, p. 175

Susan is a very rare friend, who is immensely loving, kind, and generous of spirit. She has been one of my closest and most loyal friends for many years, and her presence in my life is a true blessing. Amber is her constant companion, and the two are inseparable. I used a limited palette in this picture to create unity. The challenge here lay in distinguishing Susan's flesh tones from the color of Amber's fur.

Plate 78 – Mystical Light: Portrait of Eileen Bowden, p. 177

Eileen was a person who had a tremendous influence on my life. She taught meditation classes, which I attended for many years, in Victoria, B.C. She embodied for me the qualities of wisdom, gentleness, and love. I will always hold her close to my heart in gratitude for all the enduring truths that she taught me. I was privileged to know this great soul—and to be able to paint her portrait.

Notes

1. From the book, *The Art of Nature*, by Tim McNulty and Bruce Heinemann, Prior Publishing, Seattle, WA, 1992. Reprinted by permission of the authors.
2. Noted nature photographer and mountaineer John Dittli has spent the last thirty years photographing the mountains and deserts of the American West. You can view his work at: *www.johndittli.com*.
3. From the book, *Eckhart Tolle Findhorn Retreat*, copyright 2006 by Eckhart Tolle. Reprinted with permission of New World Library, Novato, CA, *www.newworldlibrary.com*.
4. Ibid.
5. Spoken by renowned watercolorist, Alvaro Castagnet, at an art workshop in Victoria, B.C., in 2007. Printed by permission of the artist.
6. See note #2.

"There are two ways to live your life.
One is as though nothing is a miracle.
The other is as if everything is a miracle."

Albert Einstein